PINS IN THE
LIBERAL BALLOON

PINS IN THE LIBERAL BALLOON

Sixty short essays on
the Church in the Modernist World

Francis Canavan, S.J.

A *catholic eye* book
Published by
The National Committee of Catholic Laymen
New York • New York • 1990

A *catholic eye* book
Published by The National Committee of Catholic Laymen, Inc.
150 East 35th Street, New York, New York 10016
ISBN 0-09627780-01
Library of Congress Catalog Card Number: 90-062956
Printed in the U.S.A., by BookCrafters, Chelsea, Michigan
First Printing, 1990

©Copyright 1990 by
The National Committee of Catholic Laymen, Inc.
All rights reserved.

Table of Contents

Forward/vii
Introduction/ix
1. On Being Personally Opposed/1
2. Okay Clerics for Okay Kids/5
3. Preaching by Silence/7
4. A Pluralist Church/10
5. The Loyal Opposition/13
6. The Real World/16
7. Christian Realism/19
8. Standing at Armageddon/22
9. Nearer to the Heart's Desire/25
10. The Hierarchy of Beings/28
11. Meaning in a Meaningless World/31
12. Order in the Soul/34
13. Sunset of the Enlightenment/37
14. The Pope's Dutch Treat/40
15. Vive la Différence/43
16. The Feminine Touch/46
17. Liberalism and the Catholic University/49
18. Liberalism and the Catholic University, II/52
19. The Americanization of Catholics/55
20. Selective Listening/58
21. How to Kill Freedom of Speech/61
22. Slogans for All Seasons/64
23. Argument Stoppers/67
24. Intrinsically Evil Acts/70
25. The New Sacraments/73
26. The Logic of Contraception/76
27. The Severed Link/79
28. Tadpoles and Babies/82
29. A Divorce Culture/85
30. Dissolving the Norms/88

31. Not Tea for Two/*91*
32. Infanticide/*94*
33. The Methodology is the Message/*97*
34. Taking Christmas Seriously/*100*
35. Ladies in Writing/*103*
36. Liberty, Equality, and Order/*106*
37. Lost in the Cosmos/*109*
38. Why Anything Goes/*112*
39. Papal Social Thought/*115*
40. "Imposing" Moral Beliefs/*118*
41. Civilization is for the Civilized/*121*
42. Rights as the Beginning and End/*124*
43. Equal—and Separate/*127*
44. Stooping to Folly/*130*
45. The Problem of Evil/*133*
46. Christian Freedom/*136*
47. Going to Hell/*139*
48. A Disintegrating Culture/*142*
49. Those Who Care, Govern/*145*
50. Ordered Liberty/*148*
51. Plastic People/*151*
52. Dying for Mama/*154*
53. The Rot in Liberal Politics/*157*
54. How to Read a Newspaper/*160*
55. An Uncertain Trumpet/*163*
56. The Truth about Christmas/*166*
57. The Devil We Know/*169*
58. Doing Better for Lent/*172*
59. Handling the Easy Cases/*175*
60. All of This for Me/*178*

Cover design by Paul Hebert.

The cartoon on page 39, by Mr. Douglas Hall, first appeared in the Dec. 11, 1987 issue of *Christianity Today*. All other cartoons first appeared in *The Spectator* (©The Spectator, London, England). All are reprinted here with permission.

Foreword

Some seven years ago, the Committee decided to test a publication that would be quite different from the then-available "Catholic press" fare. It would report Catholic news from what we considered an "orthodox" perspective—our own. We deliberately avoided a capital "C" to visually emphasize the point that we would make no pretense to speak for the "official" Church: *catholic eye* would be written strictly from the laymen's viewpoint.

Well, not quite: we decided to include a *Commentary* column in which we could publish the opinions of such clerics as we might want to hear from, even if they held views different from our own, provided that we thought such views would interest our readers. For our "pilot issue" (July, 1983) we asked our old friend Francis Canavan to try such a column for us. He did. And we sat back to see what kind of reaction *catholic eye* would produce. Put modestly, it was an instant success; so was Father Canavan's column. Thus we began regular publication in October, and invited Canavan to contribute regularly. With few exceptions, he has done that faithfully ever since. He has failed us in one thing only: he has yet to write a column containing "views different from our own"—not after we *read* it, anyway—he is a most persuasive man.

Soon we were getting requests to reprint his columns. We were delighted to oblige and, by now, a good many of them have appeared in a wide variety of publications, from parish bulletins to professional quarterlies.

Then we began hearing another insistent question: Why had we not published a collection of Canavan's columns? A very good question, to which this book is the answer. We asked him if he would select them for us and, as usual, he obliged us with the five dozen columns you find here. If you have not previously read them, we think you will consider them a delightful "find" indeed. We have no doubt that Canavan's regular readers will be just as delighted to have his remarkable "sermonettes" handy on their bookshelves. Lord willing, it will be followed by Canavan II in due course.

J. P. McFadden
for *catholic eye*

Introduction

It is a pleasure to introduce this collection of essays. Reading them all together (rather than one by one, as they appeared in *catholic eye*) has been a refreshing alternative to the morass of liberal literature I wade through every day, just to keep up with the "important" opinions. Having been Jesuit-educated myself, I have a special loyalty to the Jesuits, and it is gratifying to commend to the reader a Jesuit who continues the tradition of learning and vigorous intellectual debate that has so distinguished the order.

Of course, in this age, the Jesuits are known for being in the forefront of liberal movements in the Catholic Church. But not Francis Canavan. With each essay, as the title puts it, he sticks one more pin in the liberal balloon, which is full of hot air in our country and in our Church. Why the liberal balloon? Well, one can say that the essence of liberalism is one big wish that people, left on their own, will be good, that what feels good *is* good, and that the disciplines and prohibitions of earlier ages are unnecessary superstitions. It is like a big balloon buoyant with wishful thinking, and it needs to be burst (or at least brought down to earth).

The impressive thing about Canavan's essays (and each one was published in approximately the same size space—Canavan is able to be consistently precise and *concise*) is that they do stick these pins in, sharply, and yet not one is a harangue against the left. There can be no doubt about Canavan's point, yet he writes with grace and restraint. His logic and clear understanding of the Church and of his own faith cut through foggy liberal arguments much more effectively than an emotional plea. He offers an appeal to our reason. Not that these essays are without emotion—Canavan's reason is always in the light of Christ's love. As is evident especially in the final essay, "All this for Me," Father Canavan's heart is always with his head.

> Every thinking Catholic has the lifelong task of harmonizing his faith with the findings of human reason that are available in his time. He could shake off the problem, as some do, by renouncing his faith. But we are speaking of a man who wants to keep his faith, who regards it as a boon rather than a burden, and who finds that it helps rather than hinders him in understanding the world in which he lives. Nonetheless, he will have the never-finished task of bringing the teachings of faith and the conclusions of reason into a coherent and harmonious relationship: the Catholic mind is by native instinct a synthesizing mind.

This quote, from "Liberalism and the Catholic University II" (p. 52) demonstrates, I think, the importance of reading (and writing) essays such as the ones collected here. Religious faith, as we Catholics understand it, is a constant struggle to bring our intellect, our human reason, our spirituality, and our obedience to the Church into a livable synthesis. It is never an easy task. On the one hand, we are supposed to use our reason in our belief; on the other, we are asked to believe where reason fails us. We are also asked to accept the Church's authority even when our reason and some of our beliefs may be tugging in other directions, accepting in humility the fact that our reason and our spiritual sentiments may be affected by the world around us. The world has always affected the *behavior* of the faithful; in recent times, however, worldliness is affecting the Church from *within* by distorting the reason of its thinkers.

It is on this point that Canavan is most trenchant. In "A Disintegrating Culture," he writes "One need only look at the experience of liberal Protestant denominations to see what trying to keep up with the times leads to." The liberal Protestant denominations have made so many concessions to the modern culture that it no longer seems necessary to believe in anything to belong. (I recall a conversation I had with a friend, who told me about another friend of his who was studying for the ministry. He said that she was a feminist, worked as a counselor for abused women, had been in a "meaningful" lesbian relationship but was now about to enter into a more meaningful heterosexual marriage, and that she was great at analyzing dreams. . . . All these things he knew about her. I said, "Well, she *is* in an Episcopal seminary, I mean, does she believe in Christ?" *That* he did not know. It obviously wasn't something she talked about.)

Christ *is* the center of the Catholic Church. But Canavan argues that the Church will have little hope for the future if she tries to accommodate herself to dissenters, "loyal" though they may be. The point that even the dissenters would agree with is this: a church no longer willing to take a stand is not a church worth defending. Argument is inescapable, as is the tension we have between faith and reason, but it is the authority of the Church that will ensure its existence.

Even those who disagree with some of Canavan's conclusions (and God knows that in the Church today there *are* many voices and many minds) will find his essays lucid and refreshing, if only as a clarification of the "other side." And for those who *agree* with him, these essays will, I predict, produce a great sigh of relief; someone has put into clear and pleasing prose many of their own appeals to the truth. They can take comfort, in the face of galloping liberalism in our world and in our Church, that there is an eminently reasonable voice pleading their case.

MARIA MCFADDEN
for *catholic eye*

On Being Personally Opposed

In 1983, the name of Sister Agnes Mansour was much in the news. A member of the Sisters of Mercy, she had been appointed by the Governor of Michigan to administer an important State agency. Confronted with an order from the Pope himself either to quit the State post or leave the Sisters of Mercy, she chose to give up membership in her religious community. The *New York Daily News* reported her reason for leaving the community in these words:

> It was inevitable. Agnes Mansour, as she is known now, is head of the Michigan welfare and social services agency, which among other things paid 5.7 million last year . . . for 19,500 abortions for women too poor to afford them. Personally, Sister Agnes said, she opposed abortions. But, she also said, it was not fair to deny abortions to poor women as long as other women could afford them.

Since her sense of fairness triumphed over her personal opposition to abortion, Agnes Mansour departed from the Sisters of Mercy. There is no point in reviving discussion of her case now. But there is one sentence in the above report that is worth reflecting upon because so many other people have expressed the same sentiment as Miss Mansour. That is, she said she was personally opposed to abortions but thought it unfair to deny abortions to poor women when other women could afford them.

Now that is a very puzzling statement. At a first and rapid glance, it may seem to make sense. But when one pauses to think about it, the sentence becomes obscure. What does "personally opposed" mean in this context? Does it and can it mean anything at all?

A few hypothetical questions may serve to illustrate the difficulty in rendering the statement intelligible. What would be implied, for example, by saying that I am personally opposed to infanticide and suicide (or voluntary euthanasia), but if they are made legal, I consider it unfair to deny the poor the right to have these operations performed by professional medical staff in antiseptic and properly equipped facilities? To up the ante a bit, could one coherently say, I am personally opposed to torturing prisoners in jails, but if the law were to allow it, I would be willing to serve as warden of a prison in which it was done? Would it make sense to say that I am personally opposed to genocide, but if it becomes public policy to achieve racial purity through the extermination of certain ethnic groups, I will not impose my conscience on the public and will even administer the extermination program?

One can answer these questions by calling them unfair, because genocide, torture, suicide, and infanticide are not morally the same thing as abortion. Precisely. One is saying that genocide, etc., are moral crimes even when the law allows them, and that no one with a conscience can approve of them or take part in them; abortion, however, is different. But what, then, does it mean to say, I am personally opposed to abortion, but will approve, vote money for, or administer an abortion program?

It could mean that because of family upbringing or the teaching of a church, one regards abortion as a personal no-no, but not as something wrong in itself. The Catholic Church once forbade its members to eat meat on Fridays, not because there was anything inherently wrong in eating meat, but as an obligatory act of penance on the day of the week on which Jesus Christ died. It was an external law which the Church had made and could unmake. A Catholic politician could therefore honestly have said, I personally do not eat meat on Fridays because my church, for religious reasons, tells me not to, but I certainly will not try to impose this prohibition on the rest of the population—after all, eating meat on Friday is not something wrong in itself. Similarly, when a public officeholder tells us that he is personally opposed to abortion but considers it his duty to make it readily available to the poor, he may mean that he sees nothing morally wrong with abortion.

Or perhaps he would agree that abortion is morally wrong because, to his mind, morality is something idiosyncratic and subjective, a kind of hangup that some people have but others do not. ("Baptists are against the strangest things, but I am a Baptist, so I go along with them.") In this view of the matter, genocide and torture are *really* wrong and we simply may not engage in them, but abortion is only *morally* wrong and we must not impose our morality on those who do not share it.

What about suicide and infanticide? Well, of course, they are morally wrong, too, or at least most churches say they are, but in this day and age one hesitates flatly to pronounce them really wrong. They pose a delicate question for the holder of or candidate for public office. Let us not, however, be unfair to him. He devoutly believes that some things are really and truly wrong—racial and sexual discrimination spring to mind—and should be banned by law. But in our pluralistic society, he is deeply concerned to keep merely moral issues out of politics and law.

This is a public stance that we can admire (though not without a little effort) for its courage and sincerity, but it does beg certain questions. For instance, how do we tell the difference between those actions, like genocide, that are really wrong and those, like abortion, that are only morally wrong? It is an important question and one that our society must ultimately answer. The issues that arise and will continue to arise in public policy will force us to decide what, if anything, we collectively judge to be really wrong. But I doubt if we can expect an answer, or even serious thought about an answer, from people whose chief concern is to keep "moral issues" out of politics.

To return, however, to where we began, what does it mean to say that one is personally opposed to abortion but feels that in fairness abortion must be equally available to rich and poor? Only the person who says that knows what it means, and perhaps even he or she doesn't know for lack of having thought about it. The one thing of which we may be sure is this: the person who makes this statement does not see anything really wrong with abortion.

He does not consider abortion an evil thing to inflict on the unborn child who is killed or an evil for the persons who take part in killing him. Otherwise, he would be saying that it is unjust to deprive the poor of the equal opportunity to commit the real and genuine evils in which the well-to-do can afford to indulge. But that would be to lapse into incoherence and, while incoherence is a mode of speech that has certain obvious attractions for persons engaged in the difficult art of politics, we should be slow to attribute it to anyone as his internal state of mind. We must therefore take the man or woman who is "personally opposed to abortion, but . . ." as meaning "opposed, but not really." Rightly understood, "personally opposed" is a code word and a signal to the elect among the electorate. Unless the sender of the signal is himself simply confused, it means, "I'm with you; I don't see anything really wrong in abortion, either."

Okay Clerics for Okay Kids

Some years ago a woman came to see me because she had heard that I "knew something about law." Her son, it seemed, was coming up for trial in a federal court on a drug charge and she wanted legal advice about his chances. With some effort I succeeded in persuading her that she needed a real lawyer, not me. She finally accepted that but kept on talking, as distraught mothers do about their wayward children.

One of the stories she told me about her son was that once, when he was a child and had done something wrong, she told him to go into the bedroom, where there was crucifix hanging on the wall, and "tell God what you did." The kid disappeared into the bedroom and, after a while, came out again.

"Did you tell God what you did?" his mother asked.

"Yeah."

"And what did God say?"

"He said: 'It's okay, kid, forget it!'"

I hope you do not find the child's report of his conversation with God too amusingly outrageous, for it describes perfectly the mission of the modern minister of the gospel. People have problems, you see, and our function as apostles of the gospel of love is to relieve them of those problems by telling them that what they are doing or thinking of doing is okay, and not to worry about it. A remote and unfeeling clerical bureaucracy in Rome has laws against these things, but the God of love wants mercy, not sacrifice, and understanding of people's problems, not demands for obedience.

It is true, too, that in the gospel we find much about mercy and the forgiveness of sins, for God is a God of mercy, and there is more rejoicing in heaven over one sinner who repents than over ninety-nine just who do not need repentance. The gospel, however, seems to be talking about the forgiveness of real sins, of which sinners really repent. "Unless you repent, you will all likewise perish" (Luke, 13:3), for example, evidently assumes that there is something of which to repent.

Repentance is also understood to include a purpose of amendment. The most scandalously merciful passage in the four gospels

(John, 8:3-11) concludes with the words, "Neither do I condemn you. Go and sin no more."

There is a difference, then, between forgiving sins and solving problems, even though we Americans, as a nation of problem-solvers, do not like to admit it. To define a situation as a problem is implicitly to assert that it can be solved and must be solved, and this assertion is congenial to the pragmatic American way of thinking. We resent the notion that some situations can only be lived with until God in His good time enables us to change them without sinning against Him—or to abandon them in order to cease sinning.

To the problem-solving mind there are no sins, only problems to be solved. I remember once taking part in a panel discussion of abortion. Afterwards a little boy, the son of one of my opponents on the panel, came up to me and kept pressing the question, "But suppose it isn't *feasible* for people to have another child?" There are, sad to say, a lot of people whom it isn't "feasible" to keep alive, and it makes a lot of difference in what you are willing to do about that fact whether you regard it as a problem or as an occasion of possible sin.

It is also now commonly alleged in the press that about half the marriages in the United States break up and that the rate of divorce and remarriage among Catholics is about the same as in the rest of the population. I sometimes wonder how much this last statistic owes to clerics who see their mission as telling troubled souls, "It's okay, kids, forget it."

Preaching by Silence

Someone once asked the late Archbishop Fulton J. Sheen how to become a popular preacher. He replied with an ironic smile, "Talk about the sins they don't commit." Or, to put it another way, don't tell them what they'd rather not hear.

This technique makes for popularity, if that is all the preacher wants. But it is also useful to the sincere and dedicated preacher who has lost his faith in what he is supposed to teach. He does not contradict the doctrine of his church. He just doesn't mention it, and concentrates instead on those themes and causes, usually of a "progressive" nature, which he judges to be true and important.

He thus succeeds in preaching heresy, so to speak, by silence. No one can lay a glove on him, because he has denied no essential doctrine of faith, but the Christianity he preaches lacks several elements of the apostolic creed.

If theologians are loath to notice this trait in one another, others who do not claim to be Christians at all have pointed it out. Hans Blumenberg of Kiel University in Germany, for example, in his *The Legitimacy of the Modern Age* tells us that as life expectancy has lengthened and old age has become less unpleasant, interest in life after death has waned. "It appears," he says, "that even contemporary Christianity, around the world, scarcely mentions immortality any longer, and thus unintentionally has abandoned a principal element of its historical identity."

It is not clear how Blumenberg knows what contemporary Christianity, around the world, does or does not mention. He probably means that among the enlightened and advanced theologians whom he happens to meet, one does not hear much about immortality and eternal life. Still, there is something in what he says.

A highly intelligent Catholic layman gave a talk not long ago in which he made a telling remark. "Where I go to church," he said, "we never hear anything about hell. In a way, I suppose, that is understandable, but what is really surprising is that we seldom hear anything about heaven either."

As a report from the pews, that is striking. One can scarcely read a page of the New Testament without coming across the words "eternal life." The point and purpose of the life, death, and resurrection of Jesus Christ was to open for us the gates of heaven and to save us from the gates of hell, to make it possible for us to win eternal life and escape eternal exile from that life. But, at least in some parishes, it seems, we don't talk about that any more. One wonders why.

To explore the reasons for this development, however, would take us off on a tangent. What is immediately of interest is the way in which religion can change, not merely in its accidental and external forms, but in its very substance, simply by ceasing to teach what Blumenberg calls "a principal element of its historical identity." The teachers and the preachers may go on calling it Christianity, but sophisticated outsiders will notice that it is now something else.

So, too, eventually, will the people in the pews—those, that is, who are still in the pews. The others, for whose sake the preachers supposedly made the change, lest crude Christian doctrines—sin, death, judgment, heaven and hell, that sort of thing, you know—drive them away, will no longer be out there facing the pulpit. It takes a little effort to go to church, and when the church is telling you nothing that you could not hear with less effort from a TV commentator, you don't make the effort. The faithful who still come to church do it in the hope of hearing something different from what the enlightened secular world tells them. When they have been disappointed often enough, they will stop coming, too, and will go elsewhere.

The preachers, however, and those who taught them, do not really care what the people in the pews believe, for they see their task as leading the people to a more enlightened religion. As sincere men, they take seriously St. Paul's injunction to preach the word in season and out of season. The word as they understand it, however, is shorn of all pre-modern, historically conditioned, and mythological elements. One will find in this gospel no virgin birth, or physical resurrection from the dead, or real presence in the eucharist. Whether we can believe in the incarnation of God the Son or whether there is a Son distinguished from the Father and the Holy Spirit is left vague.

None of these things will be explicitly denied, unless perhaps by a pulpit orator who is both young and foolish and will therefore get himself into trouble. Older and more experienced preachers just won't mention the embarrassing Christian doctrines. If enough preachers refuse to talk about them, they will die of inanition and will fade away. Then we shall have a truly contemporary Christianity. There may be few people left to believe in it, but it will be contemporary.

Heresy-hunting, as we all know, is *passé* and went out with the Inquisition and the Holy Office. Besides, it is rather pointless in an age that is too sophisticated ever to explicate and teach an heretical doctrine. Today's Catholic, therefore, will not look for heresies that would require a pre-modern clarity of mind to formulate. He will do better in understanding what is going on if he begins to pay close attention, not only to what people say, but to what they don't say.

'*I managed to get one or two good sound bites into the Christmas sermon.*'

A Pluralist Church

Pluralism today is an "in" word. America, we are constantly told, is a pluralistic society in which no group may impose its beliefs and values on other groups, but every group's demands on society should get some satisfaction. Politics in such a society is an unending appeasement of relatively small but organized groups. No group gets everything it wants, but each group gets enough to keep it willing to play the political game, and so the game goes on forever. As the political commentators say, the system works.

But as Thomas A. Spragens, Jr., has pointed out in his *The Irony of Liberal Reason*, attributing the stability of the American political system to this "interest-group liberalism" may be an error in judgment. "In fact," he says,

> it may well be that the more fully the American polity approximates the pattern of interest-group liberalism, the more unstable it may become. To the extent that the policies of such a system are increasingly perceived as the product of purely self-interested logrolling, the more that system will be subjected to intensified demands and afflicted by loss of support. The system loses support because it loses its moral legitimacy, and intensified demands are placed on it as each group seeks to compensate for the real or imagined influence of its rivals. For both reasons, the system suffers from an erosion of its authority and, with it, a diminution of its capacity to govern effectively.

There is a lesson in this, I believe, for men of the Church as well as of the State. Bishops, religious superiors, and administrators of Catholic institutions dissipate their authority and lessen their ability to govern by trying to keep everybody happy. The temptation to listen patiently and to make concessions to organized and vociferous groups of nuns, priests, academics, homosexuals, or self-appointed "spokesmen for the laity" is understandable. One does not want to break the bruised reed or quench the smoking flax. Above all, one does not want to drive people out of the Church. But it must also be understood that the concessions made to them always exact a price in the loss of moral legitimacy.

To illustrate what I mean, the press quoted the feminist theologian, Rosemary Reuther, as saying that "the more we become feminists, the more difficult it is for us to go to church." But of course. Naturally, the more we become feminists, or Marxists, or individualists, or adherents of any other "ism," the more difficult it is for us to go to church.

Conversely, however, the more the Church becomes feminist (or Marxist, or individualist, etc.), the more difficult it is for the rest of us to go to church. More importantly, if the Church's accomodations to the demands of the ideologues are seen as a surrender to pressure-group tactics, it becomes harder for the faithful to believe in the moral authority of ecclesiastical superiors. The more often those who exercise authority in the name of Jesus Christ act like politicians in a pluralistic liberal democracy, the more they engender, not open revolt, but something that in the long run is even worse. That is a chronic, low-grade infection of disillusionment, cynicism, apathy, and loss of interest in the Church and her works.

This is not the kind of phenomenon that makes tomorrow's headlines, and it may take some years to register in the statistics of sociological surveys. But its effect on the Church is nonetheless real; it means that the Church loses the confidence of her people.

This infection among believing Catholics is also fed by the steady exploitation of religious symbols for political purposes. There may be some short-term political gain in having priests and nuns marching and waving placards. But the gain can only be for the short term. Once, perhaps twice, people may be willing to believe that the cause for which the clergy and religious demonstrate must be a serious moral cause, or they would not be leaving their ordinary roles in order to agitate for it. But when people come to see that the Roman collars and the religious habits are taken out of the closet only when activists need them in order to lend the authority of religion to political action, religious authority suffers erosion. People cease to take it seriously.

It is true that the demonstrators, the petition signers, the pressure-group tacticians may sincerely believe that the causes they serve are moral and religious, rather than merely political causes, and that they are in fact only carrying the gospel of

Christ into practice. Unfortunately, almost no one else believes it. Many years ago, before Vatican II, the Protestant theologian, Reinhold Niebuhr, remarked that Roman Catholicism had always been more successful than Protestantism in controlling its crackpots. That is no longer true, and the Catholic people know it.

The people I refer to are ordinary practising Catholics. They are men and women who believe the Catholic faith, who accept the teaching authority of the Catholic Church, who try with some consistency to live according to her teachings, and who go to Mass on Sundays. Most of them, as is the case in any large group, are not profound thinkers or articulate speakers and writers. They are neither saints, nor heroes, nor prophets. But they are the Church as it exists on earth, and if the Church has any effective authority, it is in their eyes. When the Church loses authority with them, she has lost it, for practical purposes, altogether.

For these people are not pluralists in their religion, whatever they may be in their politics or their daily social relationships. Like other Americans, they live in a pluralistic democratic political system. By and large, they accept it without much question. It might be better for the system if they did ask some searching questions about it. But however that may be, it does not follow that they want to live in a pluralist church that gives the impression of not being sure of what it teaches, or by what moral standards it expects its members to live, or whether it has the right to enforce religious discipline on its clergy.

The Church's authority is from God but its acceptance depends entirely on the faith and the confidence of the faithful. To sacrifice that to "pluralism" is not only bad theology, it is not even good politics.

The Loyal Opposition

Dissenting Catholics today like to call themselves the Loyal Opposition. The term implies that they do not cease to be good Catholics merely because they do not accept—or even actively oppose—certain teachings of the Pope and the bishops.

In fact, they would say, the idea that one needs to accept those teachings in order to be a member of the Church in good standing springs from an outmoded ecclesiology. The new and improved ecclesiology of the dissenters presents itself as an effort to "update the structure" of the Church's teaching authority. In practice, however, it is hard to distinguish this "updating" from a denial that there is in the Catholic Church a binding teaching authority. In some instances, it in effect denies that the hierarchy of bishops headed by the Pope constitutes a teaching body or, to use the Latin term, a magisterium endowed with ultimate authority in matters of faith and morals.

If there is a magisterium at all, it would seem, it belongs as much to the theologians as to the hierarchy. It is the theologians who do the Church's real thinking and, in the long run, it is the body of educated Catholics—college-trained and upwardly mobile—who will tell the teachers what they are willing to have taught to them.

This new doctrine is an ecclesiology, that is, a theory of the Church, but it comes disguised as a political theory when its proponents call themselves the Loyal Opposition. The political theory in turn is the result of certain historical developments in the British constitution.

In British parliamentary history it gradually became accepted that the king must govern through ministers, that the ministers must be chosen from a party having the confidence of a majority in the House of Commons, and that members of Parliament could oppose the policies of the king's ministers without being disloyal to the Crown. The term, "His Majesty's Opposition," was first used in the Commons in 1826. It was used in jest, and it got a laugh. But the notion that an organized opposition to the government in power was a normal and necessary part of the political system finally became an accepted principle of the British constitution.

As a political principle, the idea of a loyal opposition is a valuable one, but it comports ill with a church that professes to teach a divine revelation. "Political problems," as Edmund Burke put it, "do not primarily concern truth or falsehood. They relate to good or evil." The issues with which governments deal concern the goodness or soundness of policies. These are matters over which even intelligent men of good will can and do disagree. But a church that teaches what God has revealed, teaches it precisely as true—or it has nothing at all to teach.

The Catholic Church, of course, has policies as well as dogmas, as any institution operating in this world must have, and the policies are open to criticism. But the Church's policies must be judged in strict subordination to the truth that the Church teaches. About that truth and about the magisterium's authority to determine what it is, there can be no opposition entitled to call itself loyal.

Nonetheless, let us for the moment take the Loyal Opposition on its own essentially political terms. In a parliamentary system, when the government in power demands a vote of confidence, or when the opposition makes a motion of no confidence, the political survival of the government is at stake. If it loses in the vote of confidence, it must resign and allow the opposition to take power. A member of Parliament, therefore, must cast a vote that expresses either his confidence in the present government or his confidence in an alternative government that is waiting to take power.

If we insist on talking about the government of the Catholic Church in those terms, to whom do we give our confidence? Do we give it to the Pope and the bishops in communion with him? Or do we give it to the assortment of theologians, clerics, academics, journalists, and Church watchers who call themselves the Loyal Opposition?

It will not be enough to say that we think there is some validity in their criticisms or that we agree with some of their ideas. We are asked to express our confidence in their ability to guide and govern the Church with whatever authority they can claim in accordance with their beliefs, whatever they may be. How much confidence one is willing to put in them is a question which everyone will answer for himself. But let us all at least be clear in our own minds what question we are answering. It is who shall have the power to determine what the Church may teach as moral and religious truth.

For the real question that is raised by the Loyal Opposition is not a political one. It is the eminently theological question of who has the last word on faith and morals. It is true that popes and bishops seldom do the "original" thinking in the Church; that is not their function. What properly belongs to them is to speak the final and decisive word on what can be taught, and believed, and acted on as Catholic doctrine.

There is room in the Church for controversy and debate. But discussion in the Church always has for its aim the Church's determination of the truth. That is not arrived at through a political process, as the term, the Loyal Opposition, would lead us to believe.

It is one thing to present new interpretations of doctrine and criticism of old interpretations for consideration and possible acceptance. It is quite another to contest the hierarchy's right to decide whether they are acceptable. Those who do the latter are what we used to call Protestants. If that is what they are, we should not confuse the issue by calling them the Loyal Opposition.

The Real World

Our mother Eve ate the apple and got us all in trouble. We must not judge her harshly, for she had no mother of her own to warn her against talking to snakes. But the consequence of her folly and Adam's fall from grace has been the sad history of our race.

We therefore have good reason to believe, founded in both faith and experience, that things will never work out in this vale of tears quite as we should like them to do. Certain aspirations of the twentieth century, in particular, noble though they may be, are unlikely to be realized. Trying to make them come true, in fact, may make our situation worse instead of better.

We may wish for a world free of crime, war, poverty, ignorance, disease, and death. To reduce these evils is a goal worth working for, but to expect their elimination is to hope for a return to the Garden of Eden. It should not escape our notice that the most massive tyrannies of our century have been established by men who intended to create an earthly paradise.

Even without a crystal ball, one may venture certain predictions. We are not going to have a world peopled by altruists who are concerned as much or more with the welfare of others as with their own. A social, economic, and political order built upon the free and uncoerced cooperation of all citizens will not come into being, and no amount of change of social structures will bring it into being. Private property, however regulated for the common good, will continue to be necessary. So will police forces, courts, and jails.

It may even be that the death penalty, now widely regarded with horror, will again be generally accepted as an appropriate penalty for crime. If this happens, it will not be because bloodthirsty and benighted reactionaries have insisted on it, but because, as social controls break down, criminals will increase the number and atrocity of their violent crimes. Someone once remarked that every generation is faced with a new invasion of barbarians— its own children. In a weak and permissive society, some of the children grow up to be very barbaric indeed.

In its international relations, the world will not become

pacifist, and wishing will not make it so, even though we seem to have an unusually high number of wishful thinkers today. The Founding Fathers of our republic knew better. As Alexander Hamilton said in *The Federalist*, no. 6, "The causes of hostility among nations are innumerable. There are some which have a general and almost constant operation upon the collective bodies of society. . . . Has it not invariably been found that momentary passions, and immediate interests, have a more active and imperious control over human conduct than general or remote considerations of policy, utility, or justice?"

We have weapons today that can destroy whole countries. The weaponry of the eighteenth century had no such awesome power, but there is no evidence that advances in military technology have changed our fallen human nature from what it was when Hamilton wrote in 1787. The instruments of mass destruction make keeping the peace more imperative than ever before. They do not change the fact that the peace must be kept by and among the poor banished children of Eve and that force is ultimately controlled by force.

The unisex society will not arrive either. As the economy changes, the places taken in it by men and women will change, too. But men and women will continue to misunderstand each other because men will still be men and women will still be women, and they will vibrate as before on different emotional wavelengths. It boggles the mind to think of it, but Archie Bunker may have been smarter than Norman Lear.

Men and women, nonetheless, will still find each other as fascinating as they always have. We may agree with the feminists that men are a bad lot entirely and women would be well advised to stay away from them. No experience teaches us, however, that women will take that advice.

We might do better to go back to St. Paul's advice and notice what the feminists always overlook, that his heaviest emphasis was, not on "wives, obey your husbands," but on "husbands, love your wives." It is a fairly safe guess that most women prefer having fully grown up, responsible, and loving husbands to enjoying an equality that really means mutual independence. Human nature being what it is, it is an even safer guess that many women will not get such husbands.

They certainly will not get them or deserve them in a society that makes the emancipation of the individual its highest priority. That is another ideal that will not be realized: the individualist utopia in which everyone does his own thing and finds happiness in his own way, while tolerantly respecting everyone else's right to do the same. A society populated by porcupines, each bristling with rights, will not be a happy or a stable one, John Stuart Mill and Hugh Hefner to the contrary notwithstanding.

It would be easy to list other twentieth century aspirations that will not be achieved, but the point is already clear. There is a real world, and we are really in it, and it really does limit what we can hope to accomplish. One may reject this proposition as being too "conservative," on the ground that it assumes that the world is hopeless, and nothing can be done about it, and therefore there is no use trying to change it. But a sane conservatism knows that, as Edmund Burke put it, "we must all obey the great law of change. It is the most powerful law of nature, and the means perhaps of its conservation." Nor can a Christian, however conservative he be, regard as hopeless the human nature that Christ has redeemed. But he knows that, while grace heals the wounds of nature, it does not transmute nature into the substance of ideological dreams.

'I think it's Descartes, so it must be.'

Christian Realism

The late John Courtney Murray, S.J., once told me that at a convention he attended, a Protestant theologian said to him in a rather worried tone of voice, "I don't see how we can base a foreign policy on the Sermon on the Mount." Replied Fr. Murray, "I never thought we could."

He was right, too. One need only read the following passage from the Sermon on the Mount (Matt. 5:38-42) to see that, whatever it is, it is not a prescription for a foreign policy.

> You have heard that it was said, "An eye for an eye and a tooth for a tooth." But I say to you, Do not resist one who is evil. But if anyone strikes you on the right cheek, turn to him the other also; and if anyone would sue you and take your coat, let him have your cloak as well; and if anyone forces you to go one mile, go with him two miles. Give to him who begs from you, and do not refuse him who would borrow from you.

Even in matters closer to home than foreign policy, these words of Our Lord do not prescribe a set of rules to be followed to the letter. Anyone who has lived or worked in a parish rectory is acquainted with the stream of panhandlers, grifters, and confidence men who come to the door looking for handouts, and knows that in order to keep funds to help the really needy, it is often necessary not to give to those who beg and to refuse those who want to borrow.

We all know that civilization would collapse if we repealed the criminal law and never resisted evil men. Civilization would be in equal peril if we got rid of the civil law and saved people the trouble of suing us by immediately giving them whatever they wanted and more besides. But if we know that much, we may presume that Christ knew it, too.

We shall make more sense of the Sermon on the Mount if we do not think of it as an early edition of the Code of Canon Law or a proposal that we renounce the rule of law altogether in order to live on love alone. It is, after all, what it is usually called, a sermon. As such, it is an exhortation, not a set of rules. What it exhorts us to do is to give up certain very natural human attitudes and replace them with opposite and supernatural ones.

If we look at small children—those cute and lovable little kids—we see in them a number of unlovable attitudes which no one has to teach them. They know instinctively the difference between mine and thine, and while this does not stop them from grabbing what is thine, it makes them loudly possessive of what they regard as "mine." The urge to retaliate and to return injury for injury is also inborn and strong in them. If someone calls them a name, they have to call him a nastier one. If someone hits them, they have to hit him back. These childish propensities, if left unchecked by moral and religious training, grow and wax stronger in later life, producing antisocial monsters. Even with the best of training, few of us outgrow them entirely.

It is these selfish, possessive, and revengeful traits of our fallen human nature that the Sermon on the Mount addresses. It speaks deliberately in exaggerated and hyperbolic language because it aims at bringing about a change of mind and heart and not at laying down a fixed code of action. Our Lord does not command us to let people walk over us whenever they want. But we'll be easier to live with and we'll contribute more to civilization if our first impulse is to turn the other cheek rather than to let someone have it between the eyes. We may even say that we'll have a civilization worth defending only if it has people in it who are willing to take the Sermon on the Mount to heart.

Christians, God knows, have often made a travesty of Christian civilization. Our Christian faith carries on an unequal and frequently losing battle with our natural passions. Yet it is well for us that the battle is fought at all.

I recall something I heard from a friend of mine in the Foreign Service when I visited him in the Middle Eastern country in which he was then stationed. It was a remark the Italian ambassador to that country had made to him: "I never realized how much a Christian I am until I came here—these people don't understand mercy."

The great tyrants of our century, who slaughtered human beings by the tens of millions, have been emancipated ex-Christians like Stalin and Hitler, who dismissed the Sermon on the Mount as sentimentalism, or pagans turned atheists, like Mao Tse-Tung and Pol Pot, who possibly never heard of it. Their policies, foreign and domestic, would doubtless have been less "realistic" if they had been tempered by any degree of Christian sentiment. But how much of their kind of realism can the world stand?

Before we reject the Sermon on the Mount as hopelessly unrealistic, we ought to ask ourselves whether we should want to live in a place where everyone was of that opinion. I am thinking of a place where people constantly try to beat each other out, where everyone grabs, where no slight or injury is left without retaliation; where the highest wisdom is, don't get mad, get even; where the highest form of wit is the one-liner that leaves its victim helpless and humiliated; where, at least in certain circles and in certain parts of town, the life of man is, in the familiar phrase, solitary, poor, nasty, brutish, and short.

If you would really like to live in such a place, let me know and I'll send you a bumper sticker that reads, "I Love New York." Or, if that seems too harsh a judgment on my native city and its genial population, let me send you a neatly hand lettered sign that says simply, "Go to Hell." Hell, you know, is where no one takes the Sermon on the Mount seriously.

Standing at Armageddon

"We stand at Armageddon and we battle for the Lord," thundered Theodore Roosevelt at the Bull Moose Party convention in 1912. That was one of the more memorable lines that have been delivered in American political rhetoric. One might also describe it as archetypical. In our political idiom we stand forever at Armageddon and battle for the Lord. The republic is always in danger, the enemy is always at the gates, if not already within them, and the citadel must always be defended to the last man and (as we must now add) woman. The native style of political speech is hyperbole.

All of this is good clean fun and adds a little excitement to our otherwise dull lives. It does no great harm, either, if we do not take it too seriously, and for the most part we do not. Still, our way of talking about political issues produces a fair amount of regrettable mental confusion.

The confusion lies in this, that at one and the same time we overmoralize political issues and politicize moral issues to the point where we deny that they are moral issues at all. Which issues we moralize and which we politicize depends more on our political objectives than on any reasoned moral philosophy.

There is a sense in which every political issue is, at some outer limit, a moral one. An old saw in the literature of public administration has it that there is no Democratic and no Republican way to pave a street. *A fortiori*, there is no Christian, Jewish, Moslem or agnostic way to do it. We can say, nonetheless, that the moral way to pave a street is the one that gives the public the best road that can be obtained at the price it is willing to pay, and not the way that best lines the pockets of public officials or of their supporters in the contracting business.

There is therefore a moral principle involved even in decisions about paving streets. The principle, however, tells us nothing about the kind of materials to be used, the structure of roadbeds, or the method of building road drains. Those are engineering questions, and highway engineers can and do differ about them.

Politicians and taxpayers, too, may differ on whether we should spend more to get the best roads that can be built or spend less in order to have more money for other community needs. Those who insist that this is a purely moral issue understand neither morality nor politics, let alone engineering. On the other hand, the engineer who thinks that morality and politics have nothing to do with roadbuilding, since it is simply a question of efficiency, has failed to reflect on the further question: efficient for what? We cannot discuss the efficiency of means without discussing the ends for which they are efficient.

Moral principles, therefore, are necessary for the conduct of politics and government, but they are not enough. They are necessary because, if we pretend to be moral agents, we never can disregard our consciences on the ground that we are engaged in political rather than merely private action. As Edmund Burke once said, "There are some things a good man would not do even to save the commonwealth." We may add that there are some things a good man would not do even to save the world from population growth. But, except at such outer limits, moral principles alone will not furnish us with complete and adequate answers to questions of public policy. Political judgment also is needed.

Now, political judgment is always affected by a measure of uncertainty. We may, for example, take it as a moral given that the tax policies of a nation must be framed for the good of the whole country, not for that of a favored few alone. That does not tell us whether taxes should be cut, or raised, or remain as they are. Nor does it tell us which taxes should be cut or raised. The answers to these questions, even assuming an unrealistically high degree of dispassionate devotion to the common good, depend on long series of calculations about the future effects of any move we make in tax policy. The truth is that no one really knows what the effects will be. Some judgments about them are shrewder and sounder than others, but no one simply *knows*.

If this is true in such a dollars-and-cents calculation as taxation, it is all the more true in the general range of political issues, both domestic and foreign. These issues require decisions about large and complex matters. They depend for intelligent resolution on long and broad experience, the mastery of vast numbers of present facts, and an ability to discern future consequences. It is therefore unwise to dogmatize about them. Yet it is precisely here that the urge to dogmatize is strongest because political passion persuades us that we stand at Armageddon and battle for the Lord.

Not many years ago there were people in this country who would tell you that there are no absolute moral principles and that we should not presume to impose our principles on others, but of course the Vietnam War was absolutely immoral. Today we have people who profess not to know whether abortion takes human lives or homosexuality is a perversion. Yet they regard their political agenda as a direct deduction from the Constitution of the United States, or from the ineluctable dictates of moral conscience, or even from the gospel of Jesus Christ.

This is a fault, it must be admitted, that is characteristic of activist lawyers and clerics rather than of professional politicians. For instance, a priest told the National Council for Evangelization in 1984, "Catholics of the future will be more credible if their pro-life stance is complemented by a rejection of sexism, racism, ageism and other prejudices." He thus invited us to move from a stance where we can be sure of our ground into the swamp of a broad, sweeping, and vague egalitarianism as if it were all on the same moral plane. We might in fact be more credible if we confined ourselves to insisting that the politicians stay within certain basic moral limits, and left the rest to sound political judgments.

Nearer to the Heart's Desire

When I was in high school, I discovered Sir Edward Fitzgerald's *The Rubáiyát of Omar Khayyám*. Like many another high school student, I fell in love with it and at one time had most of it memorized. I still remember one quatrain that occurs toward the end of that long poem:

> Ah Love! could you and I with God conspire
> To grasp this sorry Scheme of Things entire,
> Would not we shatter it to bits—and then
> Re-mould it nearer to the Heart's Desire!

Now, that is heady stuff of the sort that appeals to adolescent sentimentality, and does no great harm if it stops there. It becomes highly dangerous, however, when adults take it seriously. The utopian revolutionary ideologies of our time have shown us how much damage this sentimentality can do, but they are only the political symptoms of a deeper spiritual disease.

Particularly in recent centuries, God has had a bad press for not making a better job of the world that He created. Much of modern atheism is less the result of rigorous intellectual argument than of emotional refusal to believe in the Creator of a world like this one. People cannot forgive Him for not creating the best of all possible worlds, when He could have done so.

If we reflect upon the matter, however, it becomes clear that, if there is no God, this *is* the best of all possible worlds, because it is the only possible world. In the absence of a Creator who existed before the world and had it in His power to create a different one, this world, or universe, or multiverse—put it on whatever scale you will—is the only reality there is. Having no cause outside of and above itself, the only reality that exists is the ground of whatever possibility there can be. Apart from it, no world is or ever was possible.

There is, in that case, no one to praise or blame, for no one is responsible for the universe. It just *is*, and it is what it is. As the realization of what that means sinks into men's minds, it engenders a profound sadness in them. The young and foolish may rejoice in the thought that horrified Dostoevsky, that if there is no God, everything is permitted. Fools see only that, if there is no divine judge, there is no one to stop the fun, but older heads understand that fun is not enough.

Fun is for kids and eventually palls on adults. Pagan *joie de vivre* would be easier to believe in if we could only see a little more of it. Most pagans today seem to be engaged in what the late Leo Strauss called the joyless quest for joy. The more intelligent pagans—the educated, urbane skeptics—follow Bertrand Russell's advice to build their lives on the foundation of a firm and unyielding despair. Being intelligent, they see that despair is the necessary response to a godless universe.

There surely is no use in getting angry at it. A mindless universe that evolves blindly in time and space neither knows or cares what we think of it. Indeed, there is little use even in thinking about it. If the universe is ultimately without purpose or meaning, it is simply unintelligible. It is not mysterious, like God, whose intelligibility transcends our minds, but who is fully intelligible in and to Himself. The godless universe, on the contrary, is devoid of intelligibility.

Professor Carl Becker, who was the very model of the urbane academic skeptic, explained that modern science has taught us to regard man "as little more than a chance deposit on the surface of the world, carelessly thrown up between two ice ages by the same forces that rust iron and ripen corn, a sentient organism endowed by some happy or unhappy accident with intelligence indeed, but with an intelligence that is conditioned by the very forces that it seeks to understand and control." Becker's view not only leaves human intelligence with no explanation—how did the mindless forces that rust iron and ripen corn produce mind?—but with no object.

A meaningless universe, after all, is just that: without meaning and so, in the final analysis, without intelligibility. When we have fully peeled the onion of the godless universe, we find at its center nothing at all. We cannot understand such a universe, not because it is too big for us to comprehend, but because in and of itself it makes no sense. A universe that is not the product of Intelligence offers human intelligence no object commensurate with itself. In studying such a universe, our minds finally come up against, not the plenitude of mystery, but a total lack of meaning.

To grasp that is to despair. Why despair is so attractive to so many minds today is an intriguing question that is worth pondering. But one answer we should refuse to be taken in by is that thinking men cannot believe in God. Men do not stop believing in God because they have discovered that the world is meaningless. Rather, they conclude that the world is meaningless because they have stopped believing in God. Their reasons for disbelief, no doubt, are many and various. But one of the more powerful ones is a sentimentality that will not accept the world that is as God's world.

We may dream of shattering the world to bits in order to remold it nearer to the heart's desire. But we really cannot do that and, when we try to do it, the results are disastrous. All rational thinking must begin with this world, the one that is.

We have a choice only between this world without God, in which case we despair, or this world with God, in which case life has a purpose, and therefore a meaning and a ground for hope. For the worst thing that can happen to us is not to endure this world's natural catastrophes or even man's inhumanity to man. The ultimate horror is to stare, eyes wide open, into the void.

The Hierarchy of Beings

In its December 31, 1984 number, *Time* published a lengthy review of David Lean's new film, *A Passage to India*. The review included this line from the novel by E.M. Forster on which the film is based: "Everything exists, nothing has value." It ended with the reviewer's judgment that David Lean's film is "true to its source and . . . true to our sense of the world as it echoes in the common consciousness of our times." That remark raises a fundamental question about our understanding of the nature of the world in which we live.

Let me illustrate the question with two examples. I remember several years ago reading a review of a book about Adolph Eichmann as an administrator. Eichmann, you recall, ran Hitler's extermination program, which put several million human beings to death. That the program was an organized system, and not an indiscriminate mass slaughter, meant that it needed a capable administrator.

He had to organize the roundup of people, by thousands at a time, in such a way that the rest of the population would not be unduly alarmed. He had to get them to railway stations, provide freight trains (in a nation at war, where transportation was in short supply), and ship these people to the death camps. There they had to be sorted out and processed, again in such a way that they would not foresee clearly what was in store for them. Eventually, they had to be herded into the death chambers and killed.

Having described the extermination program at length, the reviewer paused and commented that, of course, to talk about it as an administrative problem was black comedy. So indeed it was—but why? After all, we run a very similar program year in and year out in our own country. We round up herds of living creatures, ship them to slaughter houses, and systematically kill them—all so that you and I can have hamburgers for lunch and roast beef for dinner. Evidently we see a difference between killing human beings and killing cattle.

We also see differences among orders of beings that are lower than man. I once saw a TV news broadcast which included pictures of wild animals running in terror from a forest fire as flaming trees crashed around them. The broadcast did not—and surely would not—show a picture of a deer trapped under a tree in flames and screaming in agony as it burned alive. But if you did see such a picture, how would you react?

No doubt with intense sympathy ("suffering with," in the original Greek meaning of the word) for the animal's pain. But would you sympathize with the tree? Hardly. You might regret the loss of valuable timber, but it would be difficult to "suffer with" a tree, because trees do not feel pain. We see a difference, not only between men and cattle, but also between animals and plants.

The fundamental question, then, is where do we get our conviction about these differences? It is considered a sign of intellectual sophistication today to maintain that our judgment in favor of human beings over cattle is nothing more than a subjective preference for our own kind. We are human, so we read our preference into reality and assert that humans are better than cattle. In reality, however, cattle are as "good"—if that term has any objective meaning—as human beings.

The obvious differences among the many species of beings are explained as differences in degree of chemical complexity. Humans are more complex organisms than amoebas, but not essentially superior. Thought, sensation, life itself are only more complicated forms of the same chemical reactions that take place in nonliving beings.

Everything exists, nothing has value. Things just "are," and what they are has no value in itself, but only such value as our species or some other species gives it.

The alternative position is that there are real distinctions in the nature of things. "To be human" is "not to be a cow." But "to be a pig" is also "not to be a cow," yet that does not stop us from slaughtering pigs. Therefore, our judgment about the nature of reality is not only that "to be human" is "not to be a cow," but also that "to be human" means "to be superior to a cow, or a pig, or any other species of animal."

We are thus faced with an issue in that branch of philosophy which is called metaphysics. Do all beings exist basically on the same level? We can give either of two answers to that question, and it makes an enormous difference which one we give.

We can hold that all the beings which make up the universe exist on the same level. They simply are, and there is no ground in reality for saying that some of them are on higher levels of being than others. In reality there are no levels of being.

This line of thought, followed all the way through, leads to the conclusion that Adolph Eichmann was not a nice man, but there is no rational ground for believing that what he did was wrong. Strange as it may seem, I have heard men who identified themselves as Jews say just that.

Alternatively, we can hold that the universe we inhabit is a structured one in which there is a hierarchy of beings. They do not merely exist, but exist on higher and lower levels, and have distinct modes of being and action.

God, men, beasts, plants, and rocks have this in common, that they all "are," but they have their being on different levels. God is, necessarily, eternally, and perfectly, but our being is finite and contingent. The being of a deer includes the capacity for feeling pain and pleasure; the being of a tree does not.

Attaching more importance to human beings than to beasts, in this view, is not an expression of our feelings but a recognition of the structure of the real world. We may feel that it is revolting to kill baby seals, but we know that it is not the same thing as killing human babies.

Meaning in a Meaningless World

I know a man who has been living for years with a woman to whom he is not married. He is a decent, good-humored sort, but when asked, "Why don't you marry her?" he answers: "What difference would it make? Marriage is only a piece of paper."

He thinks of himself as a realist but, because he has never had formal training in philosophy, he does not know that he is an empiricist. Reality to him is what is empirically observable, what meets the eye, is heard by the ears, can be touched and felt; all else is simply imagination and emotion.

The empirically observable reality of marriage is a man and a woman living together, sharing the same bed and board, and they can do that with or without the "piece of paper" that is marriage. The imaginary bond of marriage may be emotionally satisfying, particularly to the woman, but from an empiricist point of view it adds nothing to the only reality there is, namely, what we can observe through our senses.

This kind of realism has a strong appeal to men who pride themselves on being hard-nosed and tough-minded. Determined to live with reality as they see it, they leave the hearts-and-flowers stuff to the opposite and weaker sex who, poor creatures, need to feel that life's most important relationships have meaning as well as factual content. Meaning, however, implies structure, order, and purpose, and these do not fall under the observation of the senses. The empiricist mind, therefore, cannot grasp them and regards them as unreal.

Because the empiricist view of the world lacks any objectively valid principle of order and coherence, an empiricist finds himself unable to talk about reality in consistent language. A striking example of this is the difficulty which sophisticated moderns have in talking about human life before birth.

We are all supposed to know that what is in the womb before birth is not a human being. In *Roe v. Wade*, seven justices of the U.S. Supreme Court could not bring themselves even to admit that it was actually alive, and so they referred to it as a "potential life." We, for our part, must never call it an unborn child, but rather a fetus, an embryo, a product of conception, or a blob of tissue. The only thing of which we are allowed to be sure is that killing it is not murder.

But at times the tongue slips, as happened in *Time*'s review of the film, *Fatal Attraction*. I gather from the review that in the film happily-married Dan has a weekend fling with a businesswoman named Alex. When it is over, he expects to return to his normal life with his wife and young daughter. But Alex, pregnant by Dan, won't let him go. The film ends in Dan's house, with Dan's wife, Beth, killing Alex.

"There is just one little problem," comments the *Time* reviewer. "In killing Alex, Beth also kills the child—Dan's child—inside her. The first wife saves her family by destroying the potential family of the woman who wanted to be Dan's second wife. One woman movie executive, who is disgusted by *Fatal Attraction*'s message, offers this bitter coda: 'Dan and Beth should be put on trial for the murder of Alex's unborn child.'"

What the woman executive would have said if Alex had wanted to abort the child, we do not know, and it would be unfair to guess. But you see the problem. The blob of tissue is sometimes an unborn child. Which it is depends on whether the mother wants to give birth to it. The empiricist mind must leave it up to her because, limited as it is at best to scientific observation, it cannot decide the question or talk coherently about life in the womb.

This incoherence appears even more plainly in a series of cases reported in the New York *Times*. "There have been at least 21 cases since 1981," according to the *Times*, "in which hospitals have sought court orders to override the wishes of a pregnant woman—by performing a Caesarean, detaining her against her will, or treating the fetus inside the womb." The courts granted the order in all but three cases. In one of them, in issuing an order for a Caesarean operation to save the baby from a possibly fatal infection, the judge explained: "It is one thing for an adult to gamble with nature regarding his or her own life; it is quite another when the gamble involves the life or death of an unborn infant."

It is true that such cases typically involved viable infants who could live outside the womb, and that the Supreme Court had declared in *Roe v. Wade* that the state could not proscribe abortion after viability "except when it is necessary to preserve the life or health of the mother." But in the companion case to *Roe v. Wade* the Court laid down a very broad definition of the "health" that would justify a physician in performing an abortion: his "judgement may be exercised in the light of all factors—physical, emotional, psychological, familial, and the woman's age—relevant to the well being of the patient." So we have a situation in which a woman who does not want to abort may be ordered by a court to undergo surgery or other treatment for the sake of her unborn child, but if she wants to abort even a viable child and can find a physician willing to declare that her broadly defined health requires it, the courts are powerless to defend the child.

There is clearly an incoherence in the law that permits this situation. But it is one which the law could remove by making a woman's power over an unborn child absolute in all cases. Doing that, however, would not change the deeper incoherence of the empiricist mind for which, in a world of sheer facticity, no fact, not even a human life, has intrinsic worth or any meaning save that which we choose to give it.

Order in the Soul

"In Europe during the Middle Ages, the cure of souls was public, the cure of bodies private," says Michael Walzer in his *Spheres of Justice*. "Among medieval Christians," he explains, "eternity was a socially recognized need, and every effort was made to see . . . that every Christian had an equal chance at salvation and eternal life: hence, a church in every parish, regular services, catechism for the young, compulsory communion, and so on."

One could correct Walzer by pointing out that, while medieval knowledge of medicine was primitive, the same Church which cared for souls also cared for bodies by providing for teaching and applying such medical knowledge as there was. The universities which the Church founded had Faculties of Medicine and, although medieval hospitals could do little more than keep patients warm, dry, and nourished, it was the Church that ran the hospitals. Nevertheless Walzer is right in saying that for the Middle Ages the immortal soul was more important than the mortal body.

The situation, as he also says, has been reversed as "we have lost confidence in the cure of souls, and we have come increasingly to believe, even to be obsessed with, the cure of bodies." There has been a major shift of attitude in our Western culture, with the result that "as eternity receded in the popular consciousness, longevity moved to the fore." If, after death, there is no eternal life in the next world, it becomes of supreme importance to remain alive as long as possible in this one.

But we must immediately modify that statement because our concern for longevity has not reduced the suicide rate nor will it check the growing campaign for legalized euthanasia. Modern men want, not mere life, but life in health. The health, moreover, must not only be physical but psychological. Life, to be worth living, must not only be long and healthy but also enjoyable, as the current discussion of AIDS reveals.

Our contemporary culture, officially at least, does not care what kind of sexual activity you engage in so long as you don't smoke cigarettes while doing it. Smoking, you see, is dangerous to your health. So is promiscuous sexual intercourse because it is the chief means of transmitting AIDS. The way to avoid getting AIDS would therefore seem to be "no sex" but our society instead promotes "safe sex," which supposedly allows the promiscuous to eat their cake and have it too.

We may infer from this that health is not modern society's *summun bonum* or highest good to which all other goods must be subordinated. Greatly though our society values health and however much money we are willing to spend on it, health is desirable less for its own sake than as the necessary condition for that subjective state of satisfaction that is our true end in life. The highest human good, then, is pleasure.

Yet we may doubt this proposition, too, on the ground that there is no *summum bonum*, no highest good which can serve as the organizing goal for the life of man individually and collectively. The only goal of life is a negative one: the flight from pain.

Jean le Rond d'Alembert expressed this belief at the high tide of the Enlightenment in his introduction to the famous *Encyclopedia* of Diderot which was published in Paris in 1751. "Such is the misfortune of the human condition," he wrote, "that pain is our most lively sentiment." Instead of wasting time trying to define the highest good and supreme end of human life, he concluded, philosophers "would have known our nature better if they had been content to limit their definition of the sovereign good of the present life to exemption from pain." Progress, on this view of life, becomes a movement away from pain and from those things that cause pain, chief among which are poverty and disease. It does not consist in pursuing the good.

The movement away from known evils rather than toward a knowable and objective good has been characteristic of the modern idea of progress. We can agree on what we are trying to get away from—starvation, polio, cancer, AIDS, etc,—but we find it impossible to agree on where we are trying to go.

If we add to poverty and disease such psychological states as boredom, frustration, and resentment as causes of pain, we begin to understand why alcoholism, drug abuse, and compulsive sex are increasing rather than fading out in the progressive societies. Those who become enslaved to these addictions are indeed pursuing pleasure, but they pursue it so avidly in order to fill an inner emptiness that has become too painful to live with. In a more subtle way the same may be, and often is, true of those major sources of disorder in society, the craving for wealth and the drive for power.

If one reads the "social encyclicals" of the modern popes, beginning with Leo XIII's *Rerum Novarum* in 1891, one is struck by their repeated insistence that there will be no cure for the disorders of society unless men return to belief in God as their supreme goal and final end. The popes, of course, have been voices crying in the wilderness, easily dismissed by both Left and Right as unrealistic. Yet we must ask if they are not right in this: there is no order either in the individual soul or in society without an ordering principle, and that can only be a valid purpose in life. The only adequate purpose is attaining a true and supreme spiritual good; all other purposes fail and produce disorder if they are taken as ultimate. The care of souls really is more important than the care of bodies.

Sunset of the Enlightenment

One way of describing the present state of Western culture is to say that we are living through the fag end of the Enlightenment. The late Crane Brinton, writing in *The American Historical Review* more than 25 years ago, depicted the beginning of that epoch in our culture in these terms: "The basic structure of Christian beliefs survived, not without heresies and schisms, until, roughly, the late seventeenth century when there arose in our society what seems to me clearly to be a new religion, certainly related to, descended from, and by many reconciled with, Christianity. I shall call this religion," said Brinton, "simply Enlightenment, with a capital *E*."

The Enlightenment was indeed descended from Christianity in several respects, its humanitarianism for example, yet it was nonetheless an all-out revolt against Christianity. Peter Gay, an avowed partisan of the Enlightenment, states in his *The Enlightenment: An Interpretation*: "The most militant battle cry of the Enlightenment, *écrasez l'infâme,* was directed against Christianity itself, against Christian dogma in all its forms, Christian institutions, Christian ethics, and the Christian view of the world." It was not just a Christian heresy.

The Enlightenment, in fact, attacked not only Christianity but all revealed religions, Judaism in particular, and sought to replace them with a new and worldly religion of reason. The French scholar, Paul Hazard, summarized the enlightened attitude toward revealed religion wittily but well in his *The European Mind, 1680-1715*:

> No more priests, no more pastors, no more rabbis, all alike claiming to wield authority. No more sacraments, no more rites and ceremonies, no more fasting and mortifying the flesh, no more feeling that you are obliged, willy-nilly, to go to church, chapel, synagogue, or whatever it may be . . . The present age will have no more of divine wrath, divine vengeance; nor, for the matter of that, will it tolerate any divine interference in human affairs. Vague, indefinite, remote, God did not look like causing very much embarrassment. The consciousness of sin, the need for grace, the uncertainty of salvation, which

for so many centuries had been a weight on so many hearts, would trouble the sons of men no more.

The Enlightenment not only repudiated Christian doctrine but overturned Christian morals. R.R. Palmer, in his *Catholics and Unbelievers in Eighteenth-Century France*, says that Enlightenment thinkers "observed that men sought pleasure and shrank from pain, that they enjoyed the goods of this world, that they were restive under an authority that crossed their wishes, that they lived in society and could suffer or profit from their forms of government. With these facts of human nature they hoped to build an ethical system." This new ethic would combine seeking one's own pleasure with an appropriate concern for other people, and so would lead men to happiness in this world. The religious critics of the new ethic, in Palmer's opinion, "were quite correct in calling the infidels apologists for the passions."

Does all this sound like the famous "spirit of Vatican II"? Well, as Crane Brinton said, many people reconciled the Enlightenment with Christianity in a blend which we have come to call liberal Christianity, and they are still doing it. The "spirit of Vatican II" was in fact a renewal of a three-centuries-old effort to accomodate Christianity to the Enlightenment, not something new.

Nor is it new that Enlightenment should take hold among the clergy. E.E.Y. Hales, in his *Revolution and Papacy*, describes a mentality that existed "quite widely amongst the clergy" two hundred years ago on the eve of the French Revolution. Many of the clergy, he says, "had absorbed, at the universities, the fashionable philosophy of the times—so much more compelling than the definitions of the schoolmen—and with it ideas which sometimes leant towards a Rousseauistic sentimentality, sometimes rather towards rationalism, but always away from a literal acceptance of traditional Christian beliefs."

The "chief difficulty" of these liberal clerics, according to Hales, "came with the Second Person of the Trinity. His incarnation, crucifixion, resurrection, and ascension were apt to offend them. These fundamental beliefs of the Church seemed to them too concrete, literal, anthropomorphic." The liberal clergy were repelled by "the 'Jesuitical' approach to religion, with its emphasis on the personal and particular, on the Rosary, on the human personality of Our Lord or of His mother."

Christmas is the Catholic people's answer to this liberal and enlightened Christianity. The whole Church year is a celebration of the earthly life, death, resurrection and ascension of the Incarnate God. But no feast in the Church's calendar more vividly impresses the Catholic imagination as personal and particular and as a cause for rejoicing than Christmas, when the infant who was God was born of a virgin in Bethlehem. We celebrate an event that happened at a particular time and place in history, the birth of a Person whose life gives meaning and purpose to our lives and to the world in which we live.

Robert Anchor has told us in his *The Enlightenment Tradition* that the "legacy of the Enlightenment" is "a meaningless universe" in which "men must bear the responsibility for giving value to what they create and add to a world which they did not make and which will outlive them." On Christmas Day, as the sunset of the Enlightenment fades around us in the meaningless modern world, we may find comfort and joy in the faith that for us it is the dawn.

The Pope's Dutch Treat

Pope John Paul's visit to the Netherlands in 1985 is now history. In an age in which nothing is deader than yesterday evening's news broadcast, we could even call it ancient history. Nevertheless, old though it is as news, it still merits reflection and comment.

Before the Pope got to the Netherlands, *Time* remarked that the purpose of his trip was "to defend orthodox church teachings before Holland's more than 5.6 million Catholics, whose freethinking clergy have been heavily influenced since Vatican II by Calvinist individualism and Protestant independence." Calvinist individualism usually conjures up a picture of the individual soul standing alone before God, confessing its utter sinfulness and total depravity, and hoping to be saved by an inscrutable divine decree of predestination. That, however, was not quite the picture which the American press presented of Holland's neo-Calvinist Catholic clergy and lay intellectuals.

In preparation for the Pope's arrival dissidents organized public protests against his stands on contraception, abortion, clerical celibacy, and the role of women in the Church. At a demonstration in The Hague, theologian Edward Schillebeeckx proclaimed: "We are gathered here not only to show the other face of our church but to celebrate it." Displays at the dozens of booths which the demonstration's sponsors had set up showed what the other face of the Dutch church is. "Among the positions advocated," according to the New York *Times*, "were the rights of homosexuals to be given the sacraments and to become priests, permission for priests to marry, and equal roles for women in the church."

Press reports during the Pope's visit mentioned the same and similar themes of dissent. For example, in the Pope's presence, Hedwig Wasser, an official of a Catholic missionary group, asked if Catholicism could be credible "if we exclude rather than make room for unmarried people living together, divorced people, homosexuals, married priests and women." She did not explain, so far as I know, to whom the Church would be credible if it "made room" for such people. The Pope listened to her but made it clear in a later talk to Dutch youth that the Church's teachings on "marital love, abortion, sexual relations before or outside of marriage, or homosexual relations remain the standard for the Church for all time."

Except for one mention of "liberation theology," those were the only issues about which Dutch Catholics allegedly influenced by Calvinist individualism and Protestant independence appeared to be concerned when confronting the Pope. Their grievances all seem to have centered on the restraints which Catholic moral doctrine puts on the sexual appetite. One is left sadly wondering: Has the Reformation come to this?

You will understand that I am no great admirer of the Reformation. Had I been alive in 1517, I'd have voted against Martin Luther. If I had been alive and young just four hundred years ago in 1585, I'd have become a Jesuit to play my part in the Counter-Reformation. But looking back across four centuries, I have to admit that today's Catholic heirs of Calvinist individualism make the sixteenth-century reformers look awfully good.

Martin Luther, John Calvin, Ulrich Zwingli, John Knox and the rest of them may have been wrong, but at least they were wrong about high and very important theological issues. They disagreed with Catholic doctrine on such questions as sin and its effect on human nature, redemption, grace, the sacraments, the possibility of human merit, predestination, and salvation.

John Morley, the Victorian man of letters, once said that the great crime of the Reformation was that it taught men to argue about theology in the marketplace. But let us give credit where credit is due. The arguments in the marketplace four hundred years ago were on a higher plane than today's complaints about the frustration of sexual needs.

One may protest that this criticism of modern liberal Catholic thought is not only snide but unfair. Sex is not really the issue in such questions as the ordination of women. The real issue is the equality of all members of the Church. But even if we accept this reply, it is striking how rapidly the demand for equality becomes a demand for recognition of the equal worth of all sexual proclivities and desires.

It is no accident that individualism, carried all the way through, flowers in the emancipation of the sexual appetite. For some centuries the consequences of individualism were held in check—as they still are among conservative Protestants—by belief in God's law revealed in the Bible and/or in a natural moral law revealed based on our common human nature. But as faith in divine revelation and belief in reason's ability to discern the moral law dissolved in the acid of individualism, the equality of all individuals became the equality of all individual opinions. This in turn became the equality of all individual desires, because no standard higher than individual preference was left to appeal to.

Sexual desire is one of the strongest human desires, and therefore its demands come powerfully to the fore in claims to equal treatment for all individuals. For that reason the message the Pope got in Holland was that the modern, liberal Dutch Catholic (who has learned from Calvinists to think for himself) wants sexual satisfaction without moral restraints and insists that the Church should justify him in throwing off the restraints. If the Pope heard some background noise while listening to this message, it may have been the faint, whirring sound of John Calvin spinning in his grave.

Vive la Différence

There are females and there are women, as a clever writer (French, of course) once wrote. To which women could retort that there are male animals and there are men, and the male animals seem to have the men outnumbered. Both the Frenchman and the women would be right: we are all born male or female, but only some of us achieve manhood or womanhood.

Manhood and womanhood are the maturity of the human species. The basic fact is that we are human males or females. Men and women are what we become if we develop our humanity as we should. There are no people who are simply human beings devoid of sex or persons whose sex is irrelevant to their personality.

Sex is not a characteristic added on to human nature; it is a constituent part of our nature. Just so, our bodies are not additions to our souls. Human souls are the life principles of human bodies and can come into being in no other guise. We are ensouled bodies just as truly as we are embodied souls. Body and soul, together and as one thing, constitute us as human beings. But to be a living human body is to be a member of one sex or the other. Human beings don't exist except as males or females.

Aristotle held that nature always intends the male but produces the female when it falls short of the mark. His view was one way of understanding the insight that sex is a constituent element of nature. If nature is inherently sexual and nature is one, then, he thought, it must intend one sex and produce the other by accident or defect.

Too many still believe that maleness is the perfection of human nature, feminists not least among them, as their rabid resentment of the male shows. Still, it was a strange thing for a man as intelligent as Aristotle to say. It meant that nature can continue to reproduce itself only by falling short of the mark half the time.

It would seem more realistic to recognize that when we say that sex is a constituent element of human nature, we mean that it is of the essence of humanity to be divided into two sexes. Men and women are not two species but the two halves of a single species whose very nature it is to consist of two sexes.

A sexless humanity is a contradiction in terms: our humanity must realize itself in manhood or womanhood. Both are equally human. Both are necessary to the fullness of humanity, but not in the same way. The human race is not a collection of individuals who happen to be men and women but a society (or collection of societies) founded upon a relationship between men and women.

Men and women, no matter how mature and fully human they become, are and remain males and females. As we grow up, we may and we should transcend mere animality. But to outgrow being males and females would be to cease being human.

Now, to be male and female is to be complementary principles of generation or procreation. It is not merely that procreation is what we need males and females for. Procreation is what gives masculinity and femininity their meaning.

The technological mind, which rejects the notion that anything has a natural purpose, can and does aspire to finding a way of producing human beings that will eliminate the necessity of sex altogether. The ultimate technological dream is to produce living beings from inorganic matter in the laboratory. Should the technologists succeed, however, they will have not only eliminated the need for sex but destroyed its intelligibility.

For it is their roles in procreation that constitute men and women as what they are. They are two sexes—and can be human only as distinct sexes—because of their radical, built-in capacity for playing complementary roles in procreation. That is just as true of those of us who have remained celibate as of the mothers and fathers of families.

Nor are those roles only the obvious physical ones: males fertilize, women conceive and give birth. Men are men and women are women in everything they think, say and do—and, as another and even more clever Frenchman said, *vive la différence*. There are psychological differences rooted in the physical differences between men and women. They are not in the least deplorable nor should they be considered as defects to be overcome, for they are differences in affectivity rather than intelligence. Men and women never get to the stage where they are simply and merely persons. If they did, they wouldn't be human.

It is a fact of common observation that women are softer, gentler, and more sweet-tempered than men. These are admirable and lovable qualities; they are in fact the reason why men fall in love with women. They are also the qualities that suit women for mothering, as distinct from "parenting" (which is just one more attempt to deny the difference between the sexes).

The feminine qualities, it must be admitted, make it possible for men to exploit women as often as they do, sometimes ruthlessly. The remedy, however, is not to train little girls to grow up as hard as nails. It might be more difficult but in the long run it would be more truly human to train boys to appreciate and esteem womanhood as something more than mere femaleness.

We could make a beginning toward this end by reviving devotion to Mary, the virgin mother of God. Some will object to this proposal as an attempt to put women "back in their place," and so it would be, but it would also help to put the male animal in his place. It is a place in which we may hope that he will some day grow up to be a man whom women can appreciate and esteem.

The Feminine Touch

I recently made a spiritual retreat, during which I read the gospel accounts of the passion and death of Jesus Christ. I had done that many times in previous retreats, but this time something struck me to which I had not adverted before. It was that in this sad, sorry story, in which so many ignoble parts were played, none of them were played by women.

The traitor who betrayed Christ, the deserters who fled from him, the coward who denied that he knew him, the vindictive chief priests who accused him, the time-serving Roman governor who handed him over to be crucified, the brutal soldiery that tortured and executed him, the mob that derided him on the cross—all were men. In contrast, the women present appeared as ministering angels.

The only exception, and that a small one, was the servant girls of the high priest who pressed Peter to admit he was one of Christ's disciples, and so led him to deny his Master. But theirs was a minor fault and a minor part in the drama of the passion. All the other feminine parts were sympathetic or even admirable ones.

When Jesus was hauled before Pontius Pilate by the chief priests who demanded his execution, Pilate got a message from his wife: "Have nothing to do with that righteous man, for I have suffered much over him today in a dream." When Jesus walked the Via Dolorosa to Calvary, "there followed him a great multitude of the people, and of women who bewailed and lamented him. But Jesus turning to them said, "Daughters of Jerusalem, do not weep for me, but weep for yourselves and for your children." As he hung on the cross, "the women who had followed him from Galilee stood at a distance," and watched with him to the end. Other women were at his side: "Standing by the cross of Jesus were his mother, and his mother's sister, Mary the wife of Cleophas, and Mary Magdalene." When his dead body was taken down from the cross, the women left to prepare spices and ointments to anoint it, and came at dawn on Easter morning to carry out that last work of devotion. They were therefore the first witnesses to his resurrection.

All of this, however, took place long ago, at a time when women may have played sympathetic roles because they were not allowed to play important ones. If a Betty Friedan had arisen in the ancient world, two thousand years before her time, women might well have taken a more prominent part in the events of Good Friday.

It might then have been a woman who betrayed Jesus with a kiss, and another woman who denied three times that she knew him. It would perhaps have been a chief priestess who pointed a finger at Jesus and shouted: "You have heard his blasphemy. What further need have we of witnesses?" The Gospels might tell us that Pontia Pilata, Rome's first woman governor of Judea, washed her hands before the crowd and said, "I am innocent of this person's blood," then abandoned him to his executioners.

It could have been a woman's hands that pressed down the crown of thorns on the head of Christ, and women soldiers who held down his arms and legs while the nails that fastened him to the cross were hammered in. Soprano voices might have jeered at him on the cross, and have cried: "Let God deliver him now, if She wants him!"

All of these are things that might have been in a better and more enlightened age. But in fact, in a world that knew not the meaning of equality, all the dirty work was done by men.

But perhaps I am unfair in assuming that liberated and empowered women would have behaved like men. Given their due, women might have tamed power and rendered it gentle, loving, and kind. The governor of Judea might have been, not Pontia Pilata, but Shakespeare's Portia, who would have delivered a Solomonic judgment that set Jesus free and silenced his accusers.

Possibly so; there is some reason to believe it, since women are gentler and kinder than men. But there is also reason to believe that, while women may feminize power, it is more likely to masculinize *them*. Elizabeth I of England, Catherine de Medici, Queen of France, Catherine the Great, Empress of Russia, and other great ladies who sat in high places and wielded real power may win our admiration for their Machiavellian toughness, but it would be hard to love them for their femininity.

In our own century we have had Jiang Qing, the consort

of Mao Tse-Tung and later the leader of China's "Gang of Four." In an interview with a Western journalist who asked about her personal life with Mao, she said: "Sex is engaging in the first rounds. What sustains interest in the long run is power." Sex is all right for the young, but the mature woman seeks more lasting joys. She does not always find and keep them—Jiang Qing lost out in the power struggle after Mao's death—but she knows what they are and, like Lady Macbeth, will unsex herself to get them.

That is the point at issue, isn't it? Is it meaningful to speak of a woman "unsexing" herself in the drive for place and power, or is that just sexist rhetoric designed to blind women to their potentialities and keep them in their place? Is the difference between the sexes rooted in nature or produced by nurture? Are good women the same as good men, or is there a goodness appropriate to each sex? Did women behave so admirably during the passion of Christ because they were powerless, or because they were women, doing what good women naturally do?

I am inclined to believe the latter. Feminine sensibility is different from and finer than masculine sensibility, and it showed itself at its best when Jesus Christ suffered and died.

Liberalism and the Catholic University

The other day at lunch I heard someone at the next table say, "The trouble with right-wingers is, they think people who disagree with them are wicked." In contrast, we may point out, moderates (as the press calls liberals these days) regard their opponents as simply stupid.

Of the two attitudes, the moderate one is the more insulting, for a bad will can change, but stupid is forever. *Entre nous*, however, since we are all right-wingers here, let us admit that we do tend to attribute bad motives where mere muddleheadedness or the force of circumstances would suffice for an explanation.

This tendency to blame rather than to try to understand is particularly apparent when accusatory questions are asked about what is happening in Catholic institutions of higher education. The questions often assume a degree of bad will in the administrators of those institutions far greater than they are really guilty of. The situation, I believe, is much more complex.

First, it seems to me, many Catholic colleges and universities allowed themselves to get too big. Often enough they did it at the request of bishops who wanted Catholic educational programs to be available to their people in all fields and at all levels. The result, however, was a massive expansion of teaching staffs: a school can't offer a course without having someone in the classroom to teach it. The religious orders which had founded the schools found themselves outnumbered by lay faculty, many of whom were devoted Catholics, but not all of them, and a growing number were not Catholic at all.

Next, after World War II, there was an increasing emphasis on professional qualifications for university teaching; one had to have a Ph.D. in one's field. In screening applicants for teaching posts, the overriding consideration became their purely professional qualifications. Not how an applicant would fit into the faculty of a Catholic college, not what he would contribute to the college's mission, but did he have a degree from a prestigious university in molecular biology, or seventeenth-century French literature, or public policy formation was the paramount question.

At the same time, faculty power in the colleges increased greatly. The most important power in any institution is the power to hire and fire, for it shapes the institution. This power has to a large extent passed into hands of the faculty as the persons best able to judge the qualifications of new teachers. As the faculty has become less Catholic in its composition, it is less and less concerned with maintaining the Catholic character of the school. Many faculty members would regard a suggestion that they should be concerned about it as an attack on their academic freedom.

Faculty power is by no means absolute, but it is primarily the faculty in each department of a university who decide which junior teachers shall be hired, reappointed, and granted or denied tenure. Expecting college presidents or boards of trustees to "do something about it" is to misunderstand how far the colleges and universities have passed beyond their power to control.

Their power is further diminished by the proliferation of civil rights laws and judicial decisions at the federal, state, and local levels in the past two decades. As long as the American legal establishment remains mad for equality at any price, the ability of any college to choose its own faculty will be significantly limited. As for the price of equality, ask the college of your choice how much money it spent last year in legal fees to defend itself against charges of discriminating against faculty members. The answer, if you can get it, is likely to stagger you.

Where colleges have accepted government funds—and few of them have not—they have subjected themselves to an array of governmental regulations against discrimination. When you take the Queen's shilling, you have joined the Queen's army and must expect to obey orders. But, as the Grove City College case shows, even when a college refuses to take government money, bureaucrats still try to impose their regulations on it on the ground that its students, or some of them, have government loans. Yet a college that cannot exercise discrimination in staffing and governing itself progressively loses its distinctive character as a school.

It would be misleading, nonetheless, to imply that the Catholic colleges and universities have been merely passive victims of an historical flood. The developments mentioned above took place in a period in which upwardly mobile American Catholics felt an enormous yearning to be accepted by the larger society in which they lived and worked. Whether they wanted to join the country club or to be recognized by their academic peers in other universities, they put themselves under pressure to conform. What Catholic academics conformed to was the secular liberal model of a university.

They overlooked the essential distinction between academic excellence and that particular model of a university—a model no older than the Enlightenment. George Bernard Shaw's famous jibe that a Catholic university is a contradiction in terms is valid if—but only if—we build liberalism and the liberal conception of truth into the definition of a university. Many Catholic academics, both clerical and lay, however, did not pause to ask why we must make liberalism part of the definition of a university.

They simply took it for granted and tried to carry Catholic water on one shoulder and liberal water on the other. Naturally, a lot of the water got spilled, especially from the Catholic bucket. But that is a topic which must await further comment in another column.

Liberalism and the Catholic University, II

Every thinking Catholic has the lifelong task of harmonizing his faith with the findings of human reason that are available in his time. He could shake off the problem, as some do, by renouncing his faith. But we are speaking of a man who wants to keep his faith, who regards it as a boon rather than a burden, and who finds that it helps rather than hinders him in understanding the world in which he lives. Nonetheless, he will have the never-finished task of bringing the teachings of faith and the conclusions of reason into a coherent and harmonious relationship: the Catholic mind is by native instinct a synthesizing mind.

But if establishing a coherent worldview based on both faith and reason is a project for the individual Catholic, then the project can be institutionalized. What one can and must do for himself, he may do in cooperation with others. A Catholic university therefore can be conceived of as an institution designed to enable Catholics collectively to address the intellectual problems which any one of them has to face individually.

Such an institution is built upon a commitment to the truth of the Catholic religion. It does not have to enter into the question whether its religion is true before it can begin its work. The institution exists for persons who have already answered that question on grounds which they find satisfactory; persons who do not find them satisfactory presumably will go to other institutions. This institution is for those who want to move on to the further questions which arise out of what is believed by faith, what is known or speculated about by reason, and the relationship between the two.

It does not follow that a Catholic university is an insitution dedicated primarily to studying and teaching revealed religion, or that its purpose is indoctrination. To perform its task, it must study and teach all the subjects that make up the ordinary curriculum of universities in its time and place. It is through the study of these subjects that the members of the university will confront that rationally known reality which they wish to understand in the light of faith and in whose light faith itself must be interpreted. A relation, after all, always has at least two terms. If one wishes to reflect on the relationship between physics and theology, for instance, it is as necessary to know physics as it is to know theology.

A Catholic university, furthermore, cannot do its work properly unless it studies and teaches these subjects objectively—but "objective" is not a synonym for "neutral," "agnostic," or "value-free." It means only that the first intellectual duty of any man, believer or non-believer, is to understand the *real* as it is, to the best of his ability, without distorting it to fit his general view of the world.

There is an unresolvable contradiction between this model of a Catholic university and the liberal model which is commonly considered to be the only one appropriate to a free and pluralistic society. Pluralism, in this view, connotes a wide diversity of beliefs held by individuals, all of whom are equal. But to found a university on a particular belief is to give that belief a privileged position in the university. It is therefore to deny the equality of all individuals because it denies the equality of their beliefs, and so it is an attack on pluralism.

The proper name for this theory, however, is not pluralism but individualism, which is the reigning ideology of our liberal society. The liberal model of a university is a replica of the liberal society. It can rest upon no agreed body of truth, for that would limit the rights of individuals; its highest commitment can be only to the pursuit of a truth which is never to be attained. A century and a half ago, the great prophet of liberalism, John Stuart Mill, as a young man looked forward to a society which would have "convictions as to what is right or wrong, useful and pernicious, deeply engraven on the feelings by early education and general unanimity of sentiment, and so firmly grounded in reason and in true exigencies of life, that they shall not, like all former and present creeds, religious, ethical and political, require to be periodically thrown off and replaced by others." Today, when skepticism has replaced reason as the foundation of liberty, the man who wrote that line would be regarded as a fanatic intent on imposing an orthodoxy on society.

The liberal university in our day stands only for a process which is never to end in an established truth; it is by definition neutral, agnostic, and value-free. It therefore can insist only on procedural rules of scholarship which prohibit such offenses as plagiarism and falsification of evidence, but not on any substantive truth. It cannot even have a common moral code for its faculty and students. To be sure, even in a liberal university one could invite censure for committing a truly atrocious act, such as allowing oneself to be debriefed by the CIA on returning from a trip abroad, but not for a purely private fault such as leaving one's wife and children in order to cohabit with a graduate student.

In the 1977 volume of *The Journal of Church and State*, Leo Pfeffer announced that "it is only a question of time, and a comparatively short time, before Notre Dame and Fordham will be like unto Yale and Columbia." With Dr. Pfeffer, one suspects, the wish is father to the thought. But those Catholics who have accepted the liberal model of a university as normative will find it difficult to prove him wrong, if indeed they even want to do so.

'Theologians advise, I decide.'

The Americanization of Catholics

Let us lift up our eyes to the polls, whence cometh our strength. During the Extraordinary Synod of Bishops the results of a New York *Times*/CBS News Poll on the views of American Catholics were released just in time to strengthen us against any possible bad news from Rome. The *Times*' report on the poll laid it out in its opening sentence: "Majorities of American Catholics hold views that differ sharply from teachings of their church on such issues as women's ordination, divorce, birth control, and marriage for priests." On these issues Catholics are markedly more in agreement with their non-Catholic fellow citizens than with the Pope.

The pollsters gathered their data through random telephone calls to 927 Americans across the nation, of whom 280 were Catholics. The reader may ask how we can take 280 persons as representing the views of scores of millions of Catholics in the United States, but I have no answer to that question. I took a course on statistics once, but that was decades ago and I am in no position to argue with professionals who assure me that if you know 280 of them, you know them all.

Before making up my mind on the answers given by our 280 representatives, however, I'd like to know more about the questions they were asked. For example, in the summary of poll results published in the *Times*, we are told that 63 percent of all Catholics (and 67 per cent of non-Catholics) "favor letting priests marry." But what does "favor" mean?

If the question means, or was taken to mean, do you think priests should have a right to marry if they want to, I don't find an affirmative response surprising. We are Americans and as such believe in rights and little else: everyone should have the right to do what he wants to do (so long as it doesn't hurt anyone else, of course).

Suppose, however, that "favoring" the marriage of priests means that you are willing to pay tithes, i.e., ten percent of your income, in order properly to support the priest and his family along with other church expenses. Is the answer still yes? Does "favor" mean that you would attend Mass more often, confess your sins more frequently, keep the commandments more faithfully if priests were allowed to marry?

Would you expect better sermons (or homilies as we now call them), more friendly relations between priests and the laity, more devoted service by priests to parishioners? If not, then what does "favor" mean, and why are you in favor? One would like to know before coming to a conclusion based on the answer given by 63 percent of the American Catholics who were polled.

One may be even more curious about the views of the 52 percent of Catholic women who "favor women as priests." How many women want themselves to be priests? Not one in a hundred thousand, I should guess. How many women want to be able to point with pride to "my daughter the priest"? How many would attend Mass more often, confess their sins more honestly, keep God's law more earnestly than they now do, if only they could have women priests?

Or are we dealing with nothing more than a standard American reflex? In this Land of the Free, everyone should have the right to be a priest, even though I don't want to be one myself and would not be happy if one of my children did. But everyone should have the right and of course the right must belong to both sexes equally. Anything short of that would be unconstitutional.

I do hope that I don't sound cynical or even reactionary. I must point out that my remarks find some support in a comment on the poll made by David C. Leege, the director of research for a four-year study of Catholic life by the University of Notre Dame, which has arrived at some parallel conclusions. The poll indicated, he said, "that Catholics still remain very loyal to both the faith and to the Church as an institution, but that Catholics are increasingly assimilated to American cultural values." The poll data bear him out inasmuch as 79 percent of the Catholic respondents "think it is possible to disagree with the Pope on birth control, abortion, or divorce and still be a good Catholic."

The 79 per cent constitute a new sociological category. Ex-Catholics and lax Catholics we have always known, but now we have semi-Catholics or, as the sociologists call them, communal

Catholics. They love the Church, you understand, and wouldn't dream of leaving it, but they do not intend to let the Church tell them how to live. They have assimilated American cultural values which, as Dr. Leege explains, "indicate that no one holds absolute authority and that the individual is a reasonable judge of what is moral and what is conscientious."

These are the cultural values which for more than ten years have given us a birthrate lower than the rate necessary to replace the population; a divorce rate which, as *Time* magazine has phrased it, "hits 1 of every 2 U.S. marriages"; and an abortion rate which terminates one third of all American pregnancies to the number of 1.5 million abortions a year.

Time also reports: "If present trends continue, researchers estimate, fully 40 percent of today's 14-year-old girls will be pregnant at least once before the age of 20." Some 45 percent of them will have abortions and more than half of those who do not abort will have illegitimate children; 78 percent of Americans, according to a *Time* poll, "favor" teaching contraception in the schools as the answer to this situation. It would probably be too much to expect any other response in a culture in which no one has absolute authority and the individual is a reasonable judge of what is moral and conscientious.

I recall a series of articles by Harold E. Fey which appeared in *The Christian Century* 40 years ago under the title, "Can Catholicism Win America?" Mr. Fey feared that it could, but if he is still alive today, the polls should cheer him up. The Catholic Church has not converted America, but America is doing a pretty good job of converting the members of the Church.

Selective Listening

"I may attribute all the changes of religion in the world to one and the same cause; and that is, unpleasing priests." I read that line when I was a seminarian, in Thomas Hobbes's *Leviathan*, which was first published in 1651, and I took it to heart. My function as a priest would not be to drive people away from the Church by my selfishneess, greed, arrogance, and insensitivity (though no doubt I have often done just that). This resolve was constantly reinforced by seminary professors, spiritual directors, and retreat masters who urged us not to break the bruised reed or quench the smoking flax but always to be understanding and as kind as possible.

When, therefore, in later life I heard lapsed or ex-Catholics tell how they had been driven away from their religion by harsh parents, tyrannical priests, sadistic brothers, and nutty nuns, I was both outraged at the oppressors and sympathetic with the victims. Today, however, having listened to hundreds of these stories, I find them harder and harder to take seriously.

There have been, and still are, parents, priests, and teachers who make religion consist mainly in the threat of punishment. But I doubt if they are the whole explanation, or any large part of the explanation, of lapses from Catholic faith and practice. Such "explanations" leave out at least half of the story, and the more important half at that.

There is the broadcasting station and there is the receiving set. Distorted messages can result from either of the two. When the receiving set is our television and the picture becomes wavy, or when it is our radio and the sound is marred by static, we do not jump to the conclusion that the broadcasting station must be sending out a defective signal. We are more likely to blame the defect on our TV or radio and to conclude that something is wrong with the receiving mechanism.

It is only when we ourselves are the receiving set that we instinctively blame all defective and distorted signals on the broadcasting station. It does not occur to us that we are getting a bad signal because that is all we are capable of picking up.

Imagine (or remember) a stubborn, self-willed but fearful

child who wants what he wants when he wants it but lives in a world of overawing adult power. Out of the whole message that well-intentioned parents, priests, and teachers try to give him, what part will he actually hear? Too often, only the words "no" and "punishment." There is more to the message, much more, but he doesn't get it—and may never get it.

If he never listens to the complete message, he will remain an embittered ex-Catholic. If he happens to have talent, he will write novels about the horrors of a Catholic childhood, which will get favorable mention in the book review section of the Sunday newspapers. But he will never understand the religion he has rejected.

There are other Catholics who do not hate the Church and do not leave it, but who listen to it with highly selective hearing. The American press, prepping us against the Pope's exhortations, assures us that these people are now the majority of American Catholics and that they love the Church while feeling free to disagree with it.

They love the Church when it gives them a warm feeling of community, but when it makes them feel uncomfortable, they stop listening. If they can't ignore the message entirely, they blame it on the broadcasting station. It does not occur to them that there might be something wrong with their receiving sets.

This confidence in one's own judgment, journalists tell us, is highest among college-educated Catholics who have learned to think for themselves. One gets the impression, however, that when these highly intelligent college graduates think, they think about sex. The sex-related subjects of contraception, divorce, the celibacy of the clergy, and the ordination of women are the most frequently reported topics of "dissent." But it may be that these are merely the subjects on which journalists are most eager to report the views of Catholics. Besides, some enlightened Catholics do have wider interests: when they aren't thinking about sex, they think about Nicaragua.

In any case, it is always the broadcasting station that is wrong. Despite their college education—or because of it— these freethinking Catholics seem unaware that the way they think is very much the product of contemporary American culture. "The American," said the French writer, Raymond Aron, "believes that when there's a problem, there's always a solution." Contraception, remarriage after divorce, marriage for the clergy, and the ordination of women solve what have been defined as problems. The American mind, being utilitarian, screens out opposition to these solutions, just as it is beginning to screen out criticism of surrogate motherhood, genetic engineering, infanticide, and euthanasia, which also solve problems.

If you think I exaggerate, try asking a Catholic college class what they think of the Chinese government's policy of allowing only one child to a family. Notice how many of the answers are based on the utilitarian argument that China cannot afford more than one child per family. Then ask yourself what chance a broadcasting station has against receiving sets like that.

'Well, it will get them into church at least twice in a lifetime.'

How to Kill Freedom of Speech

Does the liberal mind have a death wish? It gives every evidence of being driven by such a suicidal urge, but it may only be the victim of its own mistaken judgment. If the latter is the case, the mistake it makes is clear: it has abandoned reason as the foundation of liberty and has substituted skepticism.

The liberal flight from reason is beautifully exemplified in a column by Henry Mitchell which appeared in the Washington *Post* under the title, "*Playboy* and the Realm of Religion." Mr. Mitchell said in his column that he was disturbed, which seems to be the normal emotional condition of liberal journalists. What disturbed him in this particular column was the news that a major drugstore chain had decided to discontinue selling *Playboy*.

Mr. Mitchell hastens to tell us that he himself never bought a copy of *Playboy*, which assures us that he is no sex maniac. But neither are we to take him for a prude: he has counted on seeing a copy of *Playboy* lying on someone's desk or finding it in his barber shop. He thus strikes the balance we expect in a man of the world who enjoys his modicum of sexual stimulation but is not so desperately in need of it that he has to pay for it.

So it was not the news that a drugstore chain would no longer sell a magazine he didn't buy anyhow that got Mr. Mitchell's liberal juices flowing. No, it was the coincidental announcement that the Vatican was asking the Rev. Charles Curran of the Catholic University of America to recant certain of his views on sexual morals. By a natural association of ideas, Mr. Mitchell saw that the drugstore chain had yielded to moral pressure, therefore to religious prejudice.

You see, in the liberal universe which the Mitchell mind inhabits, moral judgments are and must be religious prejudices which have no rational basis. "We all know people," he says, "who would die before eating a cow or a pig or drinking a Coke or a gibson, because such things offend their religion." Crazy people, obviously, and their religions are all on the same level of insanity whether they forbid eating pork or drinking Coca-Cola.

Also on the same level of irrationality are the "many religious people" who "oppose pornography" and by whom "*Playboy* is considered pornographic." These fanatics go so far as to deny that readers buy *Playboy* for "its articles by the best-known serious writers of the nation" and assert that the only motive for buying it is "its raunchy advice on how to score and its pictures of girls."

Mr. Mitchell's only comment on the pictures is that "some say they are art, some say no." At this point you may begin to wonder if he actually ever has paged through a copy of *Playboy*, even in his barber shop. But you must remember that he is a columnist, not an art critic, and may well think it prudent to abstain from artistic judgment. You must also remember that his real point is that no rational judgment on pictures, or on art and literature generally, is possible.

Reason has nothing to do with such subjects because they are matters of taste and can be nothing more. Therefore certain people's feeling that pornography is offensive is only the way they feel about it and should have no influence on other people's right to buy it.

We cannot even allow any distinctions to be made among levels of taste which would classify some tastes as high, others as low; some as noble, others as base; some as truly human, others as degraded and degrading. There is no standard that reason can recognize by which we can make such distinctions.

The great liberal advocates of freedom of speech and press—Milton, Spinoza, and John Stuart Mill—argued for the liberty to utter our thoughts and to read the thoughts of others on exactly opposite grounds. They saw freedom of speech and press as the necessary condition for pursuing truth, virtue, and the welfare of the community. Their faith in reason may have been exaggerated, but they certainly had it. They believed that freedom to speak and publish would liberate reason to pursue rational and moral goals, not that reason couldn't recognize a moral goal if it saw one.

"Who kills a man kills a reasonable creature, God's image," said Milton in *Areopagitica*, "but he who destroys a good book, kills reason itself, kills the image of God, as it were in the eye." He also defended the right of "a discreet and judicious reader" to read "bad books," but only because "he that can apprehend and consider vice with all her baits and seeming pleasures, and yet abstain, and yet distinguish, and yet prefer that which is truly better, he is the true wayfaring Christian." Whatever we may think of that argument, it at least clearly supposes our ability to distinguish vice and virtue.

We need freedom to express our views, Spinoza argues, because "human wits are too blunt to get to the heart of all problems immediately; but they are sharpened by the give and take of discussion and debate, and by exploring every possible course men eventually discover the measures they wish." Mill contended in *On Liberty* that "in an imperfect state of the human mind the interests of truth require a diversity of opinions" because he was sure that the human mind would move toward perfection through rational debate among people of different opinions.

Contemporary liberals deny the classic liberal argument for the freedom of speech and press because they fear that if they ever admitted that truth and virtue have a meaning, it could be used to restrain their freedom to read and view whatever turns them on. But in rejecting the rational and moral ground of freedom they are cutting the ground out from beneath their own feet.

Thirty-odd years ago, in his book *The Public Philosophy*, Walter Lippmann explained how skepticism undermines freedom of speech and press: "Divorced from its original purpose and justification, freedom to think and speak are not self-evident necessities. It is only from the hope and intention of discovering truth that freedom acquires such high public significance." We protect the right to utter silly words only because that is the price we pay for the right to utter true and significant words. "But when the chaff of silliness, baseness, and deception is so voluminous that it submerges the kernels of truth, freedom of speech may produce such frivolity, or such mischief, that it cannot be preserved against the demand for a restoration of order or of decency." When we let matters go that far, "it is difficult to remember why freedom of speech is worth the pain and trouble of defending it." At that point, freedom is really in danger.

Slogans for All Seasons

There is the explanation and there is the thing explained. The difference between them is a vital one because the thing explained is real but the explanation is only our effort to render it intelligible to ourselves and other people. Explanations are necessary if we are to make sense of the world, but they are not identical with the world which they explain. That is why we have different philosophies or theories about the world and its constituent parts.

Not all theories are equally valid, however, because theory is controlled by reality. Despite what Karl Marx said, the ultimate purpose of our thinking is not to change the world but to understand it. The test of a sound theory is its correspondence to a reality which we did not create and which we can change only within limits. Theory can degenerate into ideology and often does in the modern world. Ideology is not an honest effort to understand but a program of action disguised as a philosophy. We imagine some ideal state of affairs and take it as our goal. We then work up a "philosophy" of the nature of the world, of man, and of society which makes the goal both necessary and attainable.

Our ideal may be a socialist state in which everyone gets the same income, or a participatory democracy in which everyone takes part in decisions which affect his interests, or a liberal paradise in which everyone pursues his own lifestyle, or a secularist heaven on earth in which no one takes religion seriously. Or it may be all of the above at once. In any case, the ideal to be achieved dictates a theory about the world in which the ideal can and must be realized. If reality persists in getting in the way of the ideal, so much the worse for reality: we must change it.

Ideologies in turn spawn slogans. The slogans may refer to something valid and useful, like "the separation of church and state," but even then they are at best oversimplifications of reality. Most of the time they are distortions of reality designed to serve ideological ends. Sometimes they don't mean anything at all but only sound good.

The word "progressive," for example. "It will never be known," said Charles Peguy, "what acts of cowardice have been motivated by the fear of not looking sufficiently progressive." Yet the word is meaningless until we add meaning to it. It suggests movement in the right direction, but we have no idea what direction that is until we learn what goal we are progressing towards and why we should move toward it. Progressives seldom say; they just assume that everyone knows.

"Peace," "freedom," and "equality" all stand for desirable states of affairs, but they are not particularly useful terms while they remain abstractions which can mean whatever anyone wants them to mean. All men want peace but, as St. Augustine remarked, they want it on their own terms; hence the prevalence of wars. It is doubtful if anyone ever brought about peace simply by being for it or prevented war by being against war as such. On the contrary, turning "peace" into a political slogan may help to bring on a war.

Freedom is another word that signifies something of which we must all approve. For that very reason it is subject to vast abuse. Since the Civil War, no one in this country cares to admit that he is against freedom and for slavery. Sophists trade constantly on this devotion to freedom. Killing babies becomes "freedom of choice," peddling pornography becomes freedom of the press, ideologizing students becomes academic freedom, and a babble of lies, special pleading, and outright nonsense becomes the free market of ideas.

Any suggestion that what is offered in that marketplace should at least be an idea rather than a raw appeal to passion is met with cries of "Censorship!" Those who cry the most loudly, however, are not always concerned to preserve freedom of discussion. More often, discussion is what they want to prevent, and they have discovered that reciting the ritual word "censorship" is an effective way to do it.

"Chilling effect" is another good discussion stopper. So is "imposing your beliefs on others." If they don't work, the sophist will try "due process of law." If all else fails, he will tell people who disagree with him that they are wedded to beliefs which modern scholarship has shown to be "historically conditioned." That usually shuts them up and once again saves the freedom of the mind from the rednecks and the obscurantists.

Equality, too, is a subject on which it is easy to prevent any real discussion. All it takes is mouthing slogans about racism and the poor. If slogans do not come readily to mind, invective will do. This country has a sad history of real and sometimes brutal racial oppression, the effects of which last to this day. But shouting "racist" at anyone who raises questions about poverty programs is no help in addressing the real problems of America's ghettos and slums.

The poor we have always with us, and we have it from the Lord himself that whatever we have done or failed to do for them, his least brothers, we have done or failed to do it to him. That, he tells us, is the test by which he will judge us. But not everyone who says "The poor! the poor!" will enter the kingdom of heaven or deserve to be elected to public office in this world. Neither, of course, will everyone who preaches the virtues of self-reliance and free enterprise.

Slogans are useful for rallying us to a cause, but they are no substitute for thought. Sophists use them to keep us from thinking. But we can beat the sophists by insisting on being told what the slogans mean and why we should believe them.

Argument Stoppers

Freedom of speech and press, academic freedom, the pursuit of truth, pluralism, ecclesiology, and other interesting topics are much talked about these days, but they are seldom discussed in any meaningful way. In practice, their major use is not to furnish matter for discussion but to put an end to it. They are argument stoppers—words and phrases which have only to be recited and the argument is immediately over.

For, clearly, any adversary who is accused of violating academic freedom, or not appreciating pluralism, or holding an outdated ecclesiology, should put his tail between his legs and skulk off the field. If he does not leave but insists on staying around to debate, there is no point in continuing to argue with him because he has revealed a closed mind that is impervious to argument.

Academic freedom, for example, is supposed to guarantee the freedom to discuss any and all subjects. But academic freedom is not itself a subject of discussion among academics. They readily man the ramparts to defend their freedom. But they usually defend it as a given that needs no justification rather than with reasoned arguments which define the limits as well as the substance of the freedom.

Yet academic freedom could be discussed. It is a set of rights which has been established to serve certain intelligible purposes. One may therefore ask what those purposes are, what means serve them, and to what extent the purposes are in fact achieved, and what claims to academic freedom should be dismissed as spurious. We may also ask whether academic freedom is a univocal idea with a fixed, necessary, and unchangeable content that has the same meaning in every context, or whether its meaning depends on the kind of university to which the freedom is applied.

How do we know that the only permissible meaning of academic freedom is the one that prevails in secular liberal universities in the United States in the latter half of the twentieth century? Could it have a meaning adapted to the nature and self-chosen function of universities devoted to developing particular philosophies or theologies? If not, why not? These questions could be discussed, but they are not discussed because to raise questions about academic freedom is taken as an attack on it. Academic freedom, as the term is most frequently used, is an argument stopper.

So is the pursuit of truth which is alleged to be the end that academic freedom serves. One cannot help being a little amused when what goes on in universities is described baldly as the pursuit of truth. It is not that we do not know scholars of great integrity who dedicate their lives to seeking the truth in their particular disciplines. The conception of truth may be and often is narrow—truth is what is found in a test tube or comes out of a computer—but their devotion to it is genuine. But in large areas of thought, and those the most important ones for human life, academics seem to feel that commitment to truth would be incompatible with their professional integrity.

In theology, philosophy, literature, and moral, social, and political theory, ideas may be considered interesting, creative, even exciting, but only an obscurantist would make an issue of their truth. A steady stream of articles and books proposing fresh approaches and revisionist theories flows into the marketplace, stimulated in part by the need to "publish or perish" (for what is more publishable than a new revisionist view of something or other?). A stronger impetus is supplied by the primacy which a liberal society gives to freedom over truth.

Leading liberal theorists, in ethics and in politics, base their defense of liberty on skepticism. They insist that no alleged truth can be allowed to limit the individual's freedom to choose his own goals and fashion his own version of the good life. In the disciplines which most directly influence how people think, feel, and act, the liberal academy may ask, What is truth? But like jesting Pilate, it will not stay for an answer. As with academic freedom, the pursuit of truth is chiefly useful as an argument stopper; even those who don't believe truth is attainable can use its pursuit to shut up importunate questioners.

In Catholic circles it is now customary to put down critics by accusing them of nostalgia for the past, a pre-Vatican II mentality, a neo-Scholastic mode of thought, and insensitivity to "pluralism." Whatever ideas the critics rely upon as the premises of their arguments are easily disposed of as culturally conditioned, time-bound, and lacking in historical consciousness. (These are phrases, dear reader, that one learns in graduate school, and if you had gone to graduate school, you'd know them too.) One may reply that nothing is more culturally conditioned and time-bound than the secular enlightenment of our day—but the reply will not be heard because the argument is already over and the audience has gone home.

Does it follow that academic freedom, the pursuit of truth, the sociology of knowledge, pluralism, ecclesiology, and the Second Vatican Council are not to be taken seriously? No, they are serious subjects and should be seriously discussed. All that follows is that we should refuse to be buffaloed by question-begging putdowns and argument stoppers. The point we must insist on is simply that reciting certain phrases as ritual incantations does not foreclose discussion. If that point is established, we may be able to get on with intelligent argument about the important subjects behind the phrases.

Intrinsically Evil Acts

Western culture, nourished on the Bible, once believed in God's foresight and providential care of man. Today, while many of us still live on trust in God, our prevailing culture does not. Whatever bows we may make in God's direction, in our public discourse we talk as if man were alone in the world and had no providence to rely on but his own.

Granted, there was never a Golden Age of Faith in which everyone surrendered the direction of his life to God's will. The Bible itself makes clear that the sons of Adam and the daughters of Eve have been more distinguished for their unfaithfulness to God than for their humble compliance with His will. Yet in reading the personal correspondence of people in earlier centuries, one cannot but be struck by the sincere and ingenuous faith in God's providence which they so often expressed.

To take a particularly striking example, when Sir Thomas More was in prison awaiting Henry VIII's decision about his fate, he wrote to his daughter Margaret: "And therefore, my own good daughter, do not let your mind be troubled over anything that shall happen to me in this world. Nothing can come but what God wills. And I am very sure that whatever that be, however bad it may seem, it shall indeed be the best."

Modern man no longer talks that way. (Who is this guy "modern man," you ask? Well, you know: he lives on your block, he went to college, he reads *Newsweek*, and he listens to talk shows on TV.) Even if he has not become an atheist—and usually he hasn't—he has effectively stopped believing in a personal God who created and governs the world.

Now, God's providence has long been recognized as mysterious; the Bible's *Book of Job* tells us that. So much happens in this world that to us seems senseless, purposeless, and downright cruel. Yet our pious ancestors were willing to believe that it made sense to God and fitted into His plan for our ultimate good. Our reluctance to express that kind of faith reveals a profound change in the modern mentality.

In his *Natural Right and History* the late Leo Strauss explains what happened:

> The theological tradition recognized the mysterious character of Providence especially by the fact the God uses or permits evil for his good ends. It asserted, therefore, that man cannot take his bearings by God's providence but only by God's law, which simply forbids man to do evil. In proportion as the providential order came to be regarded as intelligible to man, and evil came to be regarded as evidently necessary or useful, the prohibition against doing evil lost its evidence. Hence various ways of action which were previously condemned as evil could now be regarded as good.

According to the theological tradition, man must accept what happens in history as God's will but he cannot take his bearings by it. We do not understand the mysterious ways in which God guides history to His ends, and so we cannot justify evil actions on the ground that they advance His plans. Our duty is simply to obey His moral will and leave the ultimate results of history to Him.

It was the German philosopher Hegel, above all, who taught the West that philosophy can discern the divine plan in history. Consequently, he said, those who on moral grounds have resisted the working out of that plan may "stand higher in moral worth than those whose crimes have been turned into the means of realizing the purposes" that God intends, but their moral worth is only "a formal rectitude deserted by the living Spirit and by God." Alexander the Great, Julius Caesar, and Napoleon committed crimes on the grand scale but they were justified because, albeit unwittingly, they furthered God's plans.

Karl Marx denied the existence of God but, taught by Hegel, he thought he knew the laws by which history necessarily operates. He therefore thought he knew the goal toward which history is inexorably moving: the classless society. He concluded that no actions are good or bad in themselves but are good or evil insofar as they hasten or impede the coming of the classless society.

The skeptical West, unlike the Marxist East, is no longer confident that we know the laws of history, but it has clung to the notion that no action is right or wrong, good or bad in itself. Now the West feels that, not only do we not understand nor can we trust God's providential will for us, we do not know and therefore cannot obey His moral will either. We are here as on a darkling plain and must find our way through this world by our own light.

This post-Hegelian and post-Marxist skepticism has lately dawned on certain Catholic intellectuals as a new revelation. A typical example of their thinking is a letter to *Time* from Jerome A. Welch, publisher of *Catholicism Today*, in which he defends the Rev. Charles Curran's "valid objections to traditional Roman Catholic positions, including those on natural law and intrinsically evil acts, contraception, sterilization, homosexuality, masturbation, abortion and divorce." In opposition to this view, Pope John Paul II insists that "there exist acts which are always and everywhere in themselves illicit," and derives this proposition from "the metaphysics of creation which is at the center of all Christian thinking." In these conflicting statements on whether actions can be intrinsically and by their nature evil we see the fundamental issue in moral theology today, and we know how it got to be an issue.

The New Sacraments

The sacraments of the new law are three: contraception, abortion, and divorce. Progressive theologians are still debating whether premarital sex, homosexual relations, and euthanasia deserve sacramental status. What the remaining sacrament might be that is needed to fill out the traditional number of seven, is a question it is best not to let the mind dwell on, at least for the present.

To put the matter in that way, however, while it may be clever, is not really fair. It assumes that the secular sacraments of our age rest upon a carefully thought out theory developed by serious thinkers. On the contrary, what educated public opinion today regards as sacred and absolute depends for the most part on no theory at all but on a set of attitudes.

One could analyze these attitudes, and point out the assumptions behind them, and explain how there is a theory of man and society implicit in them. But it would be a mistake to believe that the multitude of people who hold these attitudes—and that includes most of the spokesmen who publicly propagate them—have thought deeply about them or have any reasoned justification for them that deserves the name of theory.

It is true that a tidal wave of print about contraception, abortion, etc., has rolled off the presses. We could fill a library with books and articles that have appeared on the subject of abortion alone. Some of these publications, on both sides, are the products of hard intellectual work. But they are not the major reason for the remarkable shift in moral standards that has taken place in this and other countries in the past generation.

In the United States, insofar as the change in standards is the result of the dissemination of ideas, Hugh Hefner's *Playboy* and Phil Donahue's television show probably have had more to do with bringing it about than anything published by a university press. Ann Landers and Dear Abby reach more minds than the philosophers and theologians do. At that, even committees of The Catholic Theological Society of America have at times shaped opinion less by the force of their arguments than by their response to people's yearning to be told that what they are going to do anyhow is morally right.

Teaching is, after all, a bilateral process. No opinion-maker simply makes opinions inside other people's heads. He must have an audience that is receptive to his teaching or, at least, can be enticed, cajoled, or manipulated into being receptive. There must be something in the student to which the teacher can appeal in order to be able to teach at all.

It could be the love of truth and the desire to know. In teaching at its best, it is that to which the teacher does appeal. But it can also be the natural attitudes of what the French call *l'homme moyen sensuel*, the average sensual man.

He is no saint, obviously, but neither is he a devil who does evil for the sheer joy of doing evil. He is only human, all too human. He is the embodiment of that natural love of pleasure and dread of pain with which we are all born.

Small children live on little else. Very few human beings ever rise fully above these natural reactions and live their lives completely on their grasp of what is truly good and truly evil; when these few die, we canonize them. Most of us spend our lives in a wavering battle between our passions and our consciences. In the average sensual man, the smart money lays its bets on the passions.

Half a century ago R.R. Palmer caused something of a stir with his *Catholics and Unbelievers in Eighteenth Century France*. The conventional wisdom was—and to a large extent still is—that the eighteenth century revolt against Christianity, generally called the Enlightenment, was a triumph of reason over faith, intelligence over superstition, light over darkness. Palmer showed that the struggle was by no means so onesided, and that the Christian spokesmen had as much intelligence and were as good at argument as their unbelieving opponents.

Yet the unbelievers won and shaped the mind of the average modern man. Although they called themselves philosophers, Palmer suggests a somewhat less than philosophical reason for their victory. "Religious writers," he says, "were quite correct in calling the infidels apologists for the passions. To vindicate the emotional life against Christian doctrines of repression and abstinence, to give men the right to enjoy their natural feelings, to represent their appetites as bodily needs and legitimate parts of their personalities, all this was one of the chief aims of the philosophic campaign."

It was also one of the chief reasons for the campaign's success. The appeal of this "new morality" (which in fact is as old as humanity) is obvious. But its consequences were less clear in the eighteenth century than they are today. Voltaire, that epitome of Enlightenment reason, once wrote: "Pleasure is the object, the duty, and the goal of all reasonable beings," but he may not have foreseen where that would lead us. It is only now that we see that it involves sacramentalizing the means of removing every obstacle to that comfortably happy life which is Everyman's desire, and therefore his right, and indeed his duty.

So deeply ingrained is this conviction about the purpose of human life and about the rights and duties that flow from it, that among both the masses and the intellectuals it has ceased to be a consciously-held theory. It has settled into being an unreflecting attitude of mind that is never questioned and is furiously defended against all criticism. This mindset explains why the newspaper editorial writer, the television pundit and even, at times, the theologian reject any morality that goes against the passions of the average sensual man.

They speak nonetheless not only to us, but for us. They appeal to the weaker side of our nature, but they can do so only because it is already there. We, like them, suffer the effects of what a less enlightened but wiser age called original sin. That is why our age has a growing list of new sacraments.

The Logic of Contraception

When the encyclical *Humanae Vitae* was published in 1968, it met with a storm of protest among theologians. Two years later, in the March-April 1970 issue of *The Critic*, John Giles Milhaven remarked:

> The dissent, which was motivated by the practical needs of married people, was justified ethically by the principle that deliberately willed sexual activity need not always be open to procreation. The principle is a direct contradiction of the classic natural law principle that not only excluded any use of contraception in marriage but was also the key principle prohibiting any deliberate sex outside of marriage. So far as I know, the theologians who rejected the natural law principle in order to permit contraception have found no convincing one to replace it to prohibit all extramarital sexual behavior.

Dr. Milhaven not long afterwards left the priesthood, married a wife, and took upon himself the burdens of married people. It cannot be said, therefore, that he was unsympathetic to their practical needs. The point he made in 1970, however, remains a valid one. So far as he knew, no one then and, so far as I know, very few now have even tried to find an argument that allows contraception in marriage but prohibits all sexual activity outside of marriage. It is doubtful if those who have tried have been convincing.

Certainly they have not convinced most of the dissenters from *Humanae Vitae*. The drift of liberal theological opinion has been toward permitting premarital and even extramarital sex. Granted, as the Rev. Charles Curran has carefully explained, it must be engaged in "responsibly," for sound reasons, and only in certain circumstances. Nonetheless, the position of the theological liberals is that what makes the sexual act outside of marriage wrong is not the nature of the act, because the act has no natural and morally obliging structure and purpose. It is only the intention with which and the circumstances in which the act is performed that can make it morally impermissible.

Since liberal moral theology does not base its sexual morality on the nature of the act, it does not stop with allowing sexual intercourse, modified by contraception, both inside and outside of marriage. It also sees that the logic of contraception calls into question the idea that any particular kind of sexual act is the uniquely normal and permissible one.

Now, here is a question which is seldom confronted by pious liberals (they are the worst kind, because they piously refuse to admit unwelcome facts or to face what they regard as shocking and alarmist questions). The question is why, if it is permissible to sterilize the sexual act while performing it, it is nonetheless necessary to perform it with the organs of procreation, and with them alone. It is really no help to say that that is the only sexual act that decent Christian married couples want to perform. True enough, no doubt, but it does not tell us why other and more exotic kinds of sexual activity are wrong even for those who want to indulge in them and say that they find them helpful in cementing the bonds of love.

This is not a merely speculative academic question which may be discussed in courses on ethics and moral theology but is of no interest outside the classroom. It is, in fact, the issue that forces itself on our attention in debates on "gay rights," the transmission of AIDS, and the status of homosexuals in our society. The issue is whether homosexual relations are wrong in themselves and deserving of no protection by society or are merely the object of popular but irrational disgust.

Hardnosed liberals say flatly that there is nothing wrong with homosexual relations *per se* because no sexual relations of any kind are or can be wrong in themselves. Pious liberals confine themselves to deploring homosexual promiscuity while pleading for understanding for homosexuals. As between the two of them, we must prefer the hardnosed liberals, because they at least know what they mean and say it.

From their point of view, there is also no compelling reason why any other person at all, either of the opposite or one's own sex, need be brought into sexual activity. One may seek relief behind closed doors, with or without the help of *Playboy* and *Penthouse*, and one should not feel guilty about it. Whether it is a morally good thing to do depends entirely on one's intention and the circumstances, not on the nature of the act.

So far has liberal moral theology gone, and it was only to

have been expected. In the debate on contraception that took place in the Church of England in the 1920s, prior to the Lambeth Conference of 1930, conservative Anglicans predicted that all of the above consequences would follow from the acceptance of contraception; liberal Anglicans piously denied them. The evolution of sexual mores in the last sixty years has verified the conservatives' predictions, and the reason is not hard to see. To accept contraception as legitimate, even within marriage and for serious reasons, is to pull out the linchpin that holds the whole structure of Christian sexual morality together.

In *Humanae Vitae* Pope Paul VI restated the age-old teaching of the Church in carefully chosen words: "Each and every marriage act must remain open to the transmission of life." Whether transmission of life takes place or not—most often it does not—the openness remains the linchpin. Take it out and the structure of Christian sexual morality falls apart. In their own way, the dissenting theologians confirm that conclusion by what they are willing to accept as permissible today.

The Severed Link

You can't stop progress, can you? As the poet says, the great world spins forever down the ringing grooves of change, and only fools will try to stand in its way.

Inspired by this thought, Dr. Jack Dominian, a British Catholic psychiatrist, has written in *The Tablet* of London that the Pill has brought about "a change which is here to stay: . . . the age-old link between sexual intercourse and procreation [has been] severed for good." For this reason, he says, we need a wholly new basis for our sexual morality.

He is undeniably right in this, that the Pill will not be uninvented. But neither shall we uninvent the hydrogen bomb, chemical weapons, bacteriological warfare, electronic instruments of torture, mind-destroying drugs, modern techniques of abortion, using tissue from aborted fetuses to cure adult diseases, or advanced methods of reshaping the image of God in man through genetic engineering. All these things, too, not to mention other blessings of progress, are here to stay.

Given the fallen state of our human nature, if new technological devices exist and can be used to satisfy people's desires, people will use them. We can use technology either for good or for ill, of course. If I am alive and well and able to write this column, I owe it to modern medicine, which has preserved both my life and my eyesight. Whether that is for good or for ill, the reader may decide, but I at least am in no position to knock modern medical techniques merely because they are techniques and modern.

The problem is that, as the late John Courtney Murray, S.J., once put it, the only canon of technology is possibility. The sole question that technology answers is whether something *can* be done. Assuring us that a device is here to stay and that people will use it tells us nothing about how they should use it or whether they should use it at all. The answers to those questions must come from sources outside technology.

We live, however, in a country and an age which is reluctant to admit any external control on the use of technology because so many of us refuse to accept any moral authority superior to our own wills. For example, the morality of using nuclear weapons is a serious and seriously debated issue. But for many of our contemporaries, the issue is simply one of survival. Their reason for wanting to ban nuclear arms is not that they think that using them is in itself immoral (they have got beyond regarding anything as intrinsically immoral), but that nuclear war would end civilization as they enjoy it.

Now that technology has severed forever the link between sexual intercourse and procreation, as Dr. Dominian would have it, we must accept people's right not to have children they don't want. More recently, technology has founded a new right, people's right to have children they do want but have not been able to have through normal sexual intercourse. Their desire to have children, we hear, makes it right for them to use such techniques as artificial insemination, extra-uterine conception and surrogate motherhood. The end justifies the means, and no further questions need or may be asked.

Mankind has never been very good at controlling technological development by either religious or purely rational norms. I recall once seeing a cartoon in which one caveman shows another a bow and arrow, and explains: "This is a weapon that will end all wars." The cartoon was fictional, but it is historical fact that the Second Lateran Council in 1139 condemned the crossbow as too inhuman to use, at least against Christians. Much good that did; Christians kept on killing Christians with crossbows, and since then the development of weaponry has roared on to the point where we can now wipe out whole cities with a single blast.

Yet there is something peculiarly modern in our conviction that intense desires suffice to justify the technological means of satisfying them. Our attitude stems from what Peter Gay has called "Bacon's and Descartes' grandiose vision of man controlling nature for his own profit and delight." Knowledge is power, said Francis Bacon in the seventeeth century, and its purpose is to master nature for "the relief of man's estate." According to his younger contemporary, Rene Descartes, knowledge is "to be desired not only for the invention of an infinite number of devices that would enable us to enjoy without any labor the fruits of the earth and all its comforts, but above all for the preservation of health, which is doubtless the first of all goods and the foundation of all other goods of life."

Far be it from me to disparage either health or labor-saving devices; I enjoy them both. But we must recognize in Bacon and Descartes the beginning of a cultural shift by which the goods of the body came to be esteemed more highly than the goods of the soul. As a result, our culture is morally ill-equipped to deal with our rapidly developing technology. But let us at least grasp firmly the idea that no technique and no device is either good or bad, and no use of it right or wrong, merely because the thing has been invented and is here to stay.

Tadpoles and Babies

Is a tadpole a frog? One answer to this question is another question: Who cares? What difference does it make to us? It is not a bad answer, either, since we care no more for frogs than we do for tadpoles. Whether a tadpole is a frog may be an interesting question to some few people, but to most of us it is certainly not an important one.

It would be important, of course, to a primitive tribe that regarded the frog as a sacred animal. Frogs, to such a tribe, would be untouchable. Yet the tribe might come to feel that too many frogs were too much of a good thing. Murmurs might arise about a Frog Explosion. Something, clearly, would have to be done.

At this point the wise men of the tribe would confront the question whether a tadpole is a frog. Some of them would argue that a tadpole is not a frog because it does not look like a frog. But, they would say, looks are all we have to go by: only that is a frog which looks like a frog. A tadpole, therefore, is not a sacred animal and may be killed at pleasure.

Others among them would point out that tadpoles, if they survive, always come to look like frogs and therefore must already have the nature of frogs. Looks are not all we have to go by. We can recognize the nature of the frog as having been present from the beginning in the tadpole. To kill a tadpole, therefore, is to kill a frog.

The anti-tadpole school would probably carry the day, but not because of their superior philosophical intelligence. They would win the argument on the highly pragmatic ground that the way to get rid of unwanted frogs without feeling guilty about it is to kill tadpoles before they look like frogs.

Besides, primitive peoples tend to go by appearances and to use separate words for ice, hail, snow, rain, mist, fog, and steam because they do not recognize these apparently distinct things as different states of the same substance, water. They often take the same attitude toward embryos, infants, children, women, and men. The idea of a common and universal human nature is too abstract and sophisticated for the primitive mind.

Modern Man (the eponymous hero of our age) is nothing if not sophisticated and has risen above all that. He does not regard frogs as sacred animals. In fact, he does not believe that any animal is sacred, not even himself. From his positivistic and skeptical point of view, to argue about whether a tadpole is a frog or a fetus is a human being is beside the point.

As he sees it, we *feel* differently about the proper way to treat men, dogs, trees, and stones. But the differences are only in our feelings, not in any traits that our minds can recognize in the things themselves. To a truly modern mind, even human beings have only such worth and such rights as other human beings collectively choose to assign them. There is no natural or transcendent standard of judgment to which we can appeal to determine the worth of humanity. We may therefore make such distinctions as we choose to make among the born and the unborn, the deformed and the normal, the mentally healthy and the insane.

Such enlightened clarity of thought, however, is too strong a draught for most of the population to swallow, and so recourse to sophistry is necessary. We must talk much about rape and incest as justifications for abortion even though we know that they are the cause of very few pregnancies. We must go on endlessly about the impossibility of knowing when a fetus becomes a person, because abortion is not murder unless it kills a person. We can then quietly assume, without discussion, that a fetus, being a nonperson, may be aborted for any reason or for no reason other than the mother's will to be rid of it.

One could answer this assumption directly: we do not know that a fetus is *not* a person; therefore, to abort it is to be willing to kill it if it is a person. But even waiving that argument, we may still question the assumption that there is nothing wrong with abortion unless it is murder.

For the very least we can say is that the product of human conception is a living human being. It is a being because one does not abort nothing: something has to be in the womb to have an abortion. It is a living being because it is going through a rapid process of growth and development. This growth is not the random multiplication of cells that characterizes a tumor but a steady, progressive development into the shape and organic structure of humanity. The living thing in a woman's womb is endowed from the beginning with a uniquely human genetic program that directs its future development and constitutes it as a member of the human species. Even before it looks human it has all the biological determinants of humanity.

Whether or not it has achieved what we choose to call "personhood," there is no stage of its development at which it is an acorn striving to become an oak tree or a tadpole on the way to becoming a frog. Its development, from conception on, is simply the process by which a human being grows—as all of us did—from the initial stage of its life into the stage at which it is capable of living outside the womb.

What do we think this living human being in the womb is? That is the key question. If we start with the determination to find reasons that will justify killing it, we shall say that it is not human, or that it is not alive, or even that it is not a being—a mere "nothing" as one enthusiastic abortionist called it. Or, recognizing the weakness of all those assertions, we shall fall back on saying that it is not a person, or that no one can know if it is a person, and so we are justified in killing it when in our judgment killing is necessary, or useful, or desirable. But none of these pronouncements, however stridently made, will get us past the fact that, at bare minimum, the human embryo has a human nature and is a living human being. We wade into deep and dangerous waters when we justify killing that.

A Divorce Culture

In June 1986 the people of the Irish Republic, in a referendum, rejected a proposed constitutional amendment which would have permitted legal divorce. The London *Daily Telegraph* opined that the "massive vote against the introduction of divorce" manifested that "obsession of the Irish people with the past rather than the future" which is "both their national curse and a substantial part of their national charm." Des Hanfin, a member of the Irish Senate who led the campaign against the divorce amendment, had a briefer and more perceptive explanation: "The people did not want a divorce culture."

The key term in Senator Hanfin's comment is "culture." A culture is the set of customs, conventions, attitudes, and beliefs that shapes both the way in which people understand themselves and their society and the way in which they expect one another to act. A divorce culture not only allows divorce but affects a whole people's understanding of marriage—and their expectations of its permanence.

The liberal individualist mind, focused on the individual hard case, sees divorce only as a necessary escape hatch from a failed marriage. Such a mind does not, perhaps cannot, see the extent to which the solution to the hard case becomes the social norm, as it has become in this country, not only with divorce, but with contraception and abortion and may yet become with social acceptance of homosexuality and euthanasia.

The significant issue, however, is not whether a case can be made for some divorce, some abortion, or some euthanasia. It is whether we can maintain a society whose culture is increasingly permeated by the assumptions of liberal individualism. "For liberal individualism," Alasdair MacIntyre explains in *After Virtue*, "a community is simply an arena in which individuals pursue their own self-chosen conception of the good life, and political institutions exist to provide that degree of order which makes such self-determined activity possible." This individualism is the root from which spring our changing attitudes on the particular issues listed above.

The freedom of the individual, however, can come at a high

price for other individuals and can reshape our culture with less than happy results. Feminism, for example, is a late-blooming variety of liberal individualism, but even the feminist columnist, Joan Beck, has expressed some misgivings over the consequences of recent advances in sexual freedom for men and women alike.

"Women have been big losers in the changes in sexual mores in the last two decades," says Ms. Beck. "No-fault divorce laws, adopted in almost all states since 1970, have turned out to be enormously unfair to women and children. They have pushed millions of mothers and young children into poverty. . . . The big increase in single, female heads of households is a major reason the poverty rate remains so high."

It is a commonplace in the press today that almost one marriage in every two will end in divorce, with the consequences Ms. Beck noticed, not to mention the psychological damage done to children. In this situation it seems silly to talk as if all there were at issue was the right of autonomous individuals to escape from unhappy marriages. One could more realistically argue that the American divorce culture does not allow young people to marry in the sense of making a binding, lifelong commitment to each other, does not support them in the facsimile of marriage into which they do enter, and encourages them to break it up when the going gets tough. The culture deprives millions of young Americans of a real choice to marry.

After a while, we may expect, they will cease to care whether they marry or not. That has already happened to a large extent in Sweden, according to David Popenoe, a professor of sociology at Rutgers, the State University of New Jersey, who has been a visiting professor at the University of Stockholm. In an article distributed by the Swedish Information Service in New York, he says: "The Swedish marriage rate is now the lowest in the industrial world, and the non-marital cohabitation rate is the highest." But whether Swedish couples marry or just live together, they very often don't stay together, for "the rate of family dissolution in Sweden may also have become the highest in the industrial world."

"Many Swedes (especially younger Swedes)" says Prof. Popenoe, "see little if any significance" in "the decline in marriage and the rise of non-marital cohabitation." Some Swedish experts, he reports, attribute this indifference toward marriage to "government policy since the change in divorce laws of the early 1970's," as a result of which government is "officially 'neutral' between the two forms of living together."

Sweden's divorce rate "falls just behind that of the Western world's acknowledged divorce leader, the United States." But then, divorce assumes that a couple has been married, and in Sweden, about one quarter of all couples don't marry, and the rate of "family dissolution" is higher among non-married than married couples, so Sweden may outstrip the United States after all.

"One could think of many such non-marital unions as 'trial marriages,'" says Popenoe, "in which the step of formal marriage is taken only after the union has matured and the couple desires to signify a certain permanence to the relationship," but in fact, "the marriage rate continues to drop while the divorce rate continues to climb."

All of which suggests that the Irish voted the way they did, not because they were obsessed with the past, but because they had looked at the present in America and the future in Sweden and decided they didn't want it.

'Is this where my marriage was made?'

Dissolving the Norms

Any society with clear and strong moral standards breeds hypocrites. Unwilling or unable to live up to the socially approved norms, they pretend to do so for fear of public opprobrium. Hypocrisy is the tribute vice pays to virtue, but the hypocrites understandably resent having to pay it.

They have two avenues of escape from their uncomfortable situation. One is to change their lives and begin to practice what society preaches. The other and easier course is to undermine society's standards. In a society such as ours, which is losing confidence in its right to make moral judgments, the easy way out has become a broad highway crowded with people seeking relief from all moral rules that are not of their own choosing.

The attack on social moral standards is most obvious at the present time in the demand for "gay rights" laws. The demand succeeds as often as it does because in this country's current egalitarian mood it is hard to mobilize public sentiment against laws which only seem to forbid discrimination. But the thrust of these anti-discrimination laws is toward a deep change in social morality.

A columnist in New York's *Village Voice* has explained that the seemingly moderate campaign for an end to discrimination against homosexuals "has radical potential, because civil rights legislation opens the way to acceptance, and acceptance opens the way to dissolution of the norm." Dissolving the norm in regard to sexual conduct is the real object of the "gay rights" movement. Its purpose is to get society to agree that, in the words of another columnist, homosexuality is just another way of living and AIDS is just another way of dying.

Once society accepts this claim, further questions arise. Why, for instance, are homosexuals not allowed to marry one another? Syndicated columnist Beverly Stephen has raised this question in what may be the opening salvo of a barrage on the civil rights front.

The present structure of American marriage law, weakened though it has been in recent decades, is still heavily biased in favor of lifelong union between one man and one woman.

The law thus expresses a social judgment in favor of one way of life as against other ways, establishes a legally privileged position for heterosexual monogamy, and discriminates against people who engage in other forms of sexual union. This bias in the law deprives homosexuals of legal rights which they could enjoy if only they could get marrried.

Ms. Stephen explains: "By law, married heterosexuals have inheritance rights, tax benefits, Social Security benefits, access to a spouse's insurance coverage, and rights to make medical decisions or funeral arrangements." Unmarried couples who live together have none of these rights, but if they are heterosexuals they at least can get married. A homosexual couple cannot, and that's not fair. Ergo, we must dissolve the heterosexual norm of marriage so that everyone may enjoy equal rights.

Now, Beverly Stephen is no more an Important Thinker than you or I, and there is no need to panic merely because she has floated an idea. Still, she has allies in the upper echelons of serious thought. Bruce A. Ackerman, who is a professor of law and philosophy at Columbia University, presumably is an important thinker. At least *The Chronicle of Higher Education* takes him as one in a recent article on the revival of political philosophy. What Professor Ackerman thinks is that "our fundamental right is the right to go to hell in our own way."

Society, for Ackerman and other highly regarded academics, exists in order to protect that right: society therefore may not impose norms that impair it. Here we see the real issue that faces American society. Beneath the surface phenomena of struggles over civil rights laws, affirmative action programs, and equal protection litigation, beneath the shouting about discrimination, censorship, and "imposing values" is the question whether society can and should maintain any moral norms at all.

There are those who want to dissolve the norms in the name of liberty and equality in a pluralistic society. It becomes steadily more clear, however, that the basic premise of their argument is what George Will has aptly called the moral equality of appetites. The original American proposition was that all men are created equal and are endowed by their Creator with certain unalienable rights. Now the proposition is that all persons are equally entitled to the satisfaction of the several preferences, urges, and drives. Because the persons are equal, their appetites are equally worthy of society's moral respect and the law's protection.

Some like chocolate, some like vanilla. Some like Mozart, others prefer heavy metal. Some like girls, some like boys. Some love God, others hate Him. It is all the same because man is a bundle of desires and each man strives to satisfy the desires that he has. Society's only task is to preside over the striving with impartial neutrality so that we can all live together in peace.

As society's moral standards dissolve in the acid of this attitude, we may not succeed in keeping our domestic or international peace. I am reminded of a billboard which I often saw during World War II. It bore the picture of a particularly stupid-looking G.I., with his fatigue cap on backwards, who proclaimed, "I'm fighting for my right to boo the Dodgers." But no one fights for his right to boo the Dodgers. If you fight, you might get hurt or even killed, and in your right mind you will not risk life and limb for the sake of booing a baseball team. Nor, we may suspect, will many fight to defend an idea of liberty that dissolves every social norm worth living by or dying for.

Not Tea for Two

"Sex for one is an erotic concept whose time has come," and universal acceptance of what an earlier age called self-abuse "is the next step in civilization's sexual evolution." You didn't know that, did you? Neither did I, but now we have it on the word of no less an authority than the noted sexpert and feminist, Betty Dodson, in her new book, *Sex for One*.

But why call attention to so obviously trashy a book as this one? Who will take it seriously? Well, the audience at a Phil Donahue show might. Mr. Donahue is quoted in an advertisement for the book as saying, "In the age of AIDS, more and more people are having sex with themselves. It's certainly a lot safer! . . . It is a quite natural experience." And who, looking at a Donahue show on TV, will venture to say that his audience doesn't take him seriously and would not do the same for Ms. Dodson?

Besides, a book like this provides an answer to a question we have all asked ourselves: How far can "civilization's sexual evolution" go? At what point will the Sons and Daughters of the Sexual Revolution sit with Alexander the Great on the banks of the Oxus, weeping because there are no worlds left to conquer? The publication of *Sex for One* suggests that they are already there, because there is no farther they can go in separating sex from natural function and freeing the self from natural norms.

If this be so, we may hail the book as signaling the final triumph of liberal individualism, a climax in which the self communes with itself alone. Or, conversely, we may see it as the reduction to absurdity of the modern conception of the individual.

This last point, the meaning of individuality, is worth reflecting upon. A Jewish friend of mine, a man of eminently sound principles and conservative views, recently reminded me that Christianity has contributed significantly to individualism. He was right, and he could have reached farther back, into his own tradition, and pointed to the contribution of the Hebrew prophets.

The Old Testament presents man as created in the image and likeness of God, and for that reason as free and responsible for his actions. As a creature, man is capable of both sin and repentance, and can merit both reward and punishment. The story of the Bible, it is true, is the story of the relations between God and His often backsliding but beloved people, Israel. Yet, as the prophets made clear, in the eyes of God it is the individual who is found worthy of praise or blame, life or death.

The prophet Ezekiel, for example, proclaimed the standard of divine judgment in these terms: "I will judge you, O house of Israel, every one according to his ways, says the Lord God. . . . The son shall not suffer for the iniquity of the father, nor the father for the iniquity of the son; the righteousness of the righteous shall be upon himself, and the wickedness of the wicked shall be upon himself. . . . When a righteous man turns away from his righteousness and commits iniquity, he shall die for it. . . . Again, when a wicked man turns away from the wickedness he has committed and does what is lawful and right, he shall save his life."

That surely is a kind of individualism, but it is the individualism of a creature, not of an autonomous self-creator. In the biblical worldview, the individual human being is supremely important because he is responsible to God more than to any earthly power. Christianity carries this individualism even farther, with its doctrine of eternal life with God or eternal separation from Him as the final destiny of every human being: "It is appointed for men to die once, and after that comes judgment" (Heb. 9:27). Distasteful as the notion that man stands under God's judgment is to the modern mind, it is the source of man's worth and dignity. The individual human being can stand against the state or any other human institution because "it is necessary to obey God rather than men" (Acts 5:29). At the Last Judgment, the Lord will say to individuals, not institutions, "Come to me, you blessed" or "Depart from me, you cursed."

In this sense, we can say that the Old and New Testaments founded individualism. Yet Alasdair MacIntyre is also correct when he says in *After Virtue* that by the end of the seventeenth century, we had "that newly invented social institution, the individual." It has taken three centuries for the full implications of this new conception of the individual to work themselves out in practice, but now they are before our eyes.

There is always a time lag between the first introduction of a new idea and the full appreciation of its consequences. The newly invented individual of early modern liberal thought emerged in a culture which was still largely shaped by belief in divine revelation and natural moral law. For several generations these beliefs held in check the disintegrating effects of the new belief in individual autonomy.

But as the autonomous individual of liberal theory lost his faith in divine revelation and in the ability of reason to perceive a natural moral order, he became an independent self, a subject of rights rather than of obligations, and a sovereign will bound by no law to which he himself had not consented. In the end, he became a bundle of appetites, because his will, lacking any anchorage in a divinely-created moral order, was submerged in and identified with his desires. That, too, is a kind of individualism, but a different kind from the freedom of the sons of God, and it explains why some individuals now prefer books like Betty Dodson's to the Bible.

Infanticide

Sir Alfred Zimmern, despite his German name, was an Englishman and a professor at Oxford University. In 1911 he published what is still an excellent book, *The Greek Commonwealth*, on the culture and civilization of the pagan Greeks of the ancient world. The following long paragraph is taken from pages 330-331 of the 5th edition, published by the Oxford University Press:

> It has not been easy for admirers of the Greeks to admit that Greek theory and practice condoned the deliberate exercise of checks upon the growth of the population. Yet the evidence shows us that such was indeed the case. When a child was born it remained, by a custom universal, so far as we know, at least down to the fourth century, within the discretion of the father whether it should be allowed to live. On the fifth day after birth, at earliest, newborn infants were solemnly presented to the household and admitted to its membership. Up to the time of this ceremony the father had complete power of selection, and, what is more, it appears that this was quite frequently exercised, particularly in the case of female infants; for the provision of a dowry for his daughters weighed heavily on a Greek father's mind, and what was easier than to evade it by pleading inability at the outset? When it was decided that the infants were not to be "nourished" they would be packed in a cradle, or more often in a pot, and exposed in a public place, the poor mother, no doubt, hoping against hope, like Creusa in the *Ion*, that some merciful fellow-citizen might yet take pity on its wailing. It is strange and horrible to think that any day on your walks abroad in a Greek city you might come across a "pot-exposed" infant, as the Athenians called them, in a corner of the market-place or by a wrestling ground, at the entrance of a temple or in a consecrated cave, and that you might see a slave girl timidly peeping round to look if the child might yet be saved, or running back to bear the news to the brokenhearted young mother. For though the custom was barbarous, and promoted, if not enforced, by a barbarous necessity, the Greeks who bowed before it still remained civilized men and women. "I beg and beseech you," writes a husband in a Greek private letter which has lately returned to us from the underworld, "to take care of the little child, and, as soon as we receive wages,

I will send them to you. When—good luck to you—you bear offspring, if it is a male, let it live; if it is a female, expose it."

The world has changed, of course, since those distant pagan days. But how much the world has changed—how much have we changed—in the 20th century! In 1911 Zimmern thought that an educated audience would be shocked at the idea of putting deliberate checks on the growth of population. Seven decades later, schoolchildren are being taught by almost all the social-studies textbooks used in the public schools that they have no higher duty than checking population growth. Zimmern also assumed that modern readers would find it horrible to think that, if they could take a walk around ancient Athens, Corinth, or Thebes, they might come across infants exposed to die of starvation. Today, with more tender sensibilites, we let them starve to death in closed hospital rooms. But the babies end up just as starved and just as dead.

We don't like to talk about that: nonetheless, we are ceasing to be shocked. The mere fact that infanticide is now a controversial issue is significant. In 1911 there would have been no controversy over the proposition that killing infants through the denial of care is simply wrong and not to be done.

A profound shift in attitudes toward human life has taken place in this century, and is still going on. The legalization of abortion was a very important step in this process but, as the current discussion of the obligation to keep infants alive shows, the process is not yet finished. It fact, it has only begun.

A news report that appeared in the New York *Times* a few years ago throws a cold, clear light on our contemporary mentality: "Faced with a growing number of malpractice claims and the rising expectations of patients, a significant number of the nation's doctors have either abandoned the practice of obstetrics or are seriously considering it." In the most revealing remark in the whole report, the *Times* quoted a doctor in North Carolina who explained why he quit the field of obstetrics: "There's an attitude that says, 'We're going to have fewer babies, so we want a perfect baby.'"

Another doctor commented that unfortunately a baby doesn't always turn out perfect. "Twenty years ago it was considered an act of God. Today there are no more acts of God. They expect you should have been able to do something."

We want a perfect baby, and if we don't get one, it must be someone's fault, therefore we sue the doctor. The *Times* naturally did not mention it, but the same attitude often explains the decision to abort or to allow a deformed infant to die.

We must admit that from a purely secular point of view, killing infants makes a kind of sense. If there is no God, then there are no acts of God. If this world is the only one there is, and this life is the only one we'll ever live, why should we let our uniquely precious lives be marred by taking care of less than normally healthy children?

It is a grim kind of sense, however, and one that will appeal only to people who hold a certain view of the world and have certain expectations from it. As the less admirable features of ancient paganism re-emerge in our society, we shall indeed be more free to pursue happiness on our own terms, but it will be rough on children and other weaklings who get in our way.

The Methodology is the Message

At a political science convention which I attended some years ago, one of the speakers mentioned toward the end of his talk that the education code of every State in the Union gives the public schools a mandate to form moral character. In the discussion period that followed a young woman with a marked Southern accent protested: "Ah am shocked by what Ah just heard—it goes against everything Ah learned in graduate school!"

She had studied political science in a graduate school and had been taught a methodology based on the philosophy known as positivism. This philosophy makes a radical distinction between "facts," which can be established by the rational methods of science, and "values," i.e., judgments about good and evil, which are beyond the competence of science to establish. Since positivism recognizes only science as an exercise of reason, it regards judgments of value as expressions of feeling or emotion: to say, "this is good," means nothing more than "I approve of this," which is to say, "I like it." Political science therefore must look upon judgments about moral character as unscientific, beyond the scope of reason, and out of place in public schools.

That young lady was a good example of the kind of person who should be strongly discouraged from going to graduate school—bright enough to master a methodology but not intelligent enough to criticize it. For such people a methodology easily becomes identified with reason itself and is taken as the sole and only road to truth.

Lewis S. Feuer explains in his *Spinoza and the Rise of Liberalism*:

> Whenever a new "method" has been proposed in the history of thought, its converts and proponents have seen it as the promise of a new age. Bacon with his inductive method, Descartes with his geometrical method, Hegel's dialectical method, Spencer's evolutionary method, Russell's mathematical logic, the logical empiricists with their semantical analysis all have been regarded as prophets whose insight when extended to social and human issues would bring the final solutions. Every method has had its methodological madness.

That passage came to mind as I read "Jesus Among the Historians," an article by the Rev. John P. Meier, professor of New Testament at the Catholic University of America and general editor of *The Catholic Biblical Quarterly*, which appeared in the New York *Times Book Review* on Dec. 21, 1986. Fr. Meier went to a graduate school and learned the historical method. The purpose of his article is to explain what this method can tell us about the "historical Jesus."

He is aware, however, of the method's limitations. The "historical Jesus" is not to be identified with the Jesus who existed in time and space but is only "my fragmentary hypothetical reconstruction of Jesus through historical research," and on this reconstruction, he says, "my faith in Christ does not rise or fall." He can and does believe many things about Jesus as Christ, and believes them as true. He does not think, however, that these beliefs can be established by the scientific method of history.

One may agree with him that this recognition of the limits of science is "paradoxically liberating." It must come as a relief to realize that I am free to believe in truths that lie beyond what science can prove, precisely because the scientific method as we now understand it is so limited in what it can accomplish.

On the other hand, it is not entirely clear whether Fr. Meier fully appreciates the limits of science. The Catholic approach to the historical study of the earthly life of Jesus, he says, has one advantage over a conservative Protestant approach—"the clear distinction between what is known through historical research and reason and what is affirmed in faith. The historical Jesus belongs solely to the former realm."

One should not press a man's words too hard and make him mean what he did not intend to say. Still, one may point out that Fr. Meier's words seem to identify reason with historical research, therefore with a particular conception of both reason and scientific method. This conception has its roots in the triumphs of early modern physical science in the seventeenth century and has saddled us ever since with a particularly narrow and truncated idea of what human reason is and what it can do.

The very distinction between the Christ of faith and the Jesus of history is not of Catholic origin and did not spring from a Catholic understanding of the relationship between faith and reason. Catholic thought has always recognized the difference between what can be known by reason and what can only be accepted by faith in God's revelation. But, like the distinction between facts and values, the distinction between the Christ of faith and the Jesus of history is not one that fits easily into a Catholic mode of thought.

It was, in fact, the result of an attempt by nineteenth-century German liberal Protestants to save faith in Christ from the corrosive effects of Enlightenment rationalism. Yes, they said to the rationalists, we will give you the Jesus of history as the only one who can be rationally known, but we will keep the Christ of faith because we have never allowed reason to play a role in faith anyhow. The distinction between the Christ of faith and the Jesus of history is harmless enough if we keep clearly in mind that the Jesus of history is only the hypothetical reconstruction that can be arrived at by a certain limited methodology. But the general reader can hardly be blamed if he sees in it an invitation to choose between a Christ who cannot rationally be believed in and a Jesus who is not worth believing in. We may doubt whether that is what the New Testament has in mind.

Taking Christmas Seriously

Christmas is a scandal to the modern mind. It is not only that it has a child being born to a virgin; the greater scandal is that it has him born at all, as God entering the human race through a woman's womb. Christmas celebrates the birth of the incarnate God to a human mother whose name we know (Mary) in a place that is still there (Bethlehem), at an identifiable time in human history (when Caesar Augustus ruled the Roman Empire and Quirinius was governor of Syria). This immersion of God in historical particularity offends a mind for which, if there is a God, He should be above all that.

The Christ whose birth Christmas commemorates is presented to us as an historical figure who lived a real life in the real world, and at the end of that life was crucified, died, and rose again from the dead. The Resurrection too, however, along with all the miracles in between, is intolerable to a certain type of intellectual who wants his religion reduced to a set of "meanings" unencumbered by embarrassing assertions of fact that cannot be true and must be taken as mythological.

That Jesus was born of a virgin mother is therefore translated into a symbolic way of saying that he was an important person. That he rose again from the dead is not denied—at least, not by theologians who want to go on teaching in Catholic faculties of theology—but it is "reinterpreted" in such a way as to take it out of history. To give but one recent example, the magazine *30 Days* for September 1989, quotes the Rev. David Coffey, president of the Australian Catholic Theological Association, as saying that "the resurrection is an event of grace not involving in any way the corpse of Jesus."

We must hold, that is to say, that Jesus in some sense rose from the dead (the Creeds force us to admit that much), but his dead body did not come back to life. The historical event of his death was not followed by the equally historical event of his returning to life in the body that died on the cross. Science tells us that a corpse cannot live again, and Fr. Coffey assures us that only "in a pre-scientific age" could one believe that a corpse did that. While we must believe in the resurrection, therefore, we must also believe that it means something other than that the dead body of Jesus rose again to physical life in this world.

If this kind of theological thinking is carried all the way through, it ultimately calls into question the Incarnation itself, for it must seem strange that we can believe that God became man, but not that He was born of a virgin or that He rose from the dead. Liberal Christianity tends inexorably, as its history shows, toward Unitarianism, for which, as the quip has it, there is but one God at most. It not only takes Christ out of Christmas, it takes Him out of history altogether. All that is left in the real world in which history actually took place is the man called Jesus who lived, taught, and was executed in Palestine two thousand years ago. The rest of the Christian faith is imaginative symbolism designed to convey insights into the human condition to a myth-making age. But in our age, whose only mythology is Science, the historical Christian faith just won't do.

The outburst of art, music, and liturgy that Christmas has produced during the Christian centuries was hardly inspired by this anemic and insubstantial liberal Christianity. People do not go to midnight Mass to celebrate a birth that is merely symbolic of whatever philosophical beliefs happen to be fashionable in theological faculties. Nor do men and women become Christians if that is all that Christianity has to offer. As C. S. Lewis wrote to his friend, Malcolm, "did you ever meet, or hear of, anyone who was converted from scepticism to a 'liberal' or 'de-mythologized' Christianity? I think when unbelievers come in at all, they come in a good deal further."

Christmas is a season of joy because the Feast of the Nativity gives us something of supreme importance to rejoice about. It presupposes that we are a fallen race because of a real original sin, from the consequences of which we all need to be saved. Sin is not a popular subject, even in sermons, in an age in which religion is more and more a psychotherapy aimed at making people feel good about themselves. Yet we cannot fail to notice that the greatest horrors of our time are not the San Francisco earthquake, or Hurricane Hugo, or the tornado that ravaged Huntsville, Alabama. The worst evils we suffer are the ones we inflict on one another, on a scale we would consider massive if we had not become inured to it by seeing it every evening on the TV news.

We—all of us, and not only the obvious and flagrant bad guys—are weak, prone to sin, and in need of salvation. Without that conviction, Christmas makes no sense and gives us little joy. We rejoice because the real God became a real man and offered His life in expiation for our real sins, thereby giving us the chance to escape a real damnation and to win eternal life in a real heaven.

The tidings of great joy at Christmas are that "this day is born unto you in the city of David a Savior, who is Christ the Lord." With that announcement, Christ was born into this world. His last words to His apostles on leaving it were: "Go, therefore, and teach all nations, baptizing them in the name of the Father, and of the Son and of the Holy Spirit, . . . and lo, I am with you always even to the end of the world." Christ carries on His saving mission in historical time through His Church, and will carry it on until history comes to its appointed close.

All of these beliefs are implied in Christmas. If they are not true, the birth of Jesus from Mary in Bethlehem is insignificant. But if they are true, it is the most blessed event in history, on which the whole meaning of history turns. We have to take our Christianity straight, or it is not worth taking at all.

Ladies in Writing

A year or so from now we shall find ourselves listening to an updated set of New Testament readings at Mass. If we listen carefully, we'll notice that these readings avoid using the word "man" in any context where it refers to both the human sexes. No longer shall we hear that man does not live by bread alone; it will have become "One does not live by bread alone."

To say that man does not live by bread alone, you see, implies that woman does, because the word "man" is "exclusive." It never includes women as well as men, even though you and I and just about everyone else always thought it did.

How did this piece of ideological feminism get into our liturgy? It was put there by a committee of scholars whom the American Catholic Bishops commissioned to revise the flat and pedestrian translation of the New Testament that we have been using for liturgical readings since 1970. According to press reports, the committee has divised a more dignified and less banal translation, but it seems also to have fallen into the feminist trap.

Perhaps it would be accurate to say that it jumped in. The committee's secretary, the Rev. Stephen J. Hartdegen, says that one of the most difficult issues the committee faced was how to translate texts that were seen as "discriminating against women." To avoid this invidious discrimination, the committee resolved to use the noun, "man," and the pronoun, "he," only when referring to persons of the male sex. In so deciding, they accepted the feminist definition of "man."

It is fixed in the feminist mind that "man" means and can only mean "male." The trouble with that idea is not only that it is false. Even worse, it makes it impossible to speak English coherently. The effort to speak English as feminists would have us do leads to Henry Higgins' cry of rage in *My Fair Lady*: "By rights she should be taken out and hung for the cold-blooded murder of the English tongue!"

The original and root meaning of the syllable "man" in all the Teutonic languages was "human being," and so it remains to this day. English is exceptionl only in that precisely the same set of letters, m-a-n, denotes both the human species and the male sex of the species. (German, for example, uses two words from the same root, *Mensch*, human being, and *Mann*, male human being.) In English, "woman" is "man" with a prefix meaning "female." Only a feminist can believe that a woman is a female male; the rest of us know that she is a female man, i.e., human being.

Fr. Hartdegen knows this, too. "The generic sense of 'man' is traditional in English," he admits, but "many today reject it." Many? Some nuns, lawyers, academics, and other female yuppies reject it, that is true. But they are a relatively small class of professional people who identify themselves with their careers and have convinced themselves that allowing "man" to be used in the generic sense blocks their progress in their careers. The overwhelming majority of English-speakers of both sexes couldn't care less about "exclusive" language and will not take the trouble to speak the new "inclusive" language.

For to use feminist Newspeak consistently is a lot of trouble. We must practice an awkward, cumbersome, and ultimately silly way of speaking English in order to refer to the human species without ever using the only name we have for it: man. It is like the children's game whose point is to answer questions without using a certain word. "Green," let us say, is the forbidden word. Q.: What color is grass? A.: A shade between yellow and blue.

This is fun if we are playing a game. But it is a tiresome nuisance if we are forced, day in and day out, to resort to such barbarisms as chairperson, policeperson, fireperson, and even (God deliver us) clergyperson, or to say "he or she" every time we use the third person singular pronoun with a general reference. Yet if we are to satisfy the feminists, we must speak this clumsy and stilted language. Either that, or we must resort to endless circumlocution like the Faculty Statutes of my own university, which avoid personal pronouns by repeating the noun, "the individual," every time a pronoun would be called for. Needless to say, the Statutes read like a document drawn up by a committee of pixilated schoolteachers.

Feminists may succeed in compelling bureaucrats—who don't

speak English anyhow—to use "non-sexist" language. But why are our bishops giving in to them? The mushy-headed cleric who is all heart and no brain is a familiar figure, but he usually does not become a bishop. From bishops we may reasonably expect the intelligence to recognize nonsense when they see it and the courage to stand up to it.

The temptation of the busy administrator, however, is to placate a clamorous and persistent pressure group by making what he regards as a mere token concession to it. The row, after all, is only about a word, and the word is not worth fighting about, so let them have their word. From now on we shall not say, "Man does not live by bread alone," but "One does not live by bread alone," and that should shut these irksome ladies up.

But whether going along with them when they are making fools of themselves is really doing them a favor, and whether in fact it will shut them up, are questions whose answer only the future will reveal. In the meantime, let me suggest one more change in the liturgy: the response to the readings at Mass should be, "Speak English yet!"

Liberty, Equality, and Order

Liberty, equality, fraternity was the slogan of the French Revolution. Liberty and equality were the Revolution's operative goals, and fraternity was brought in as a cement to hold them together. For liberty and equality are not necessarily in harmony and, in fact, are often at war with each other. Keeping the peace between them therefore became the role of fraternity. Alas, fraternity has not been terribly successful at it, as the history of class struggle since the French Revolution has shown.

In the evolution of democratic theory in the past two centuries, two main currents have emerged from the same wellspring of radical individualism: the liberal stream, emphasizing liberty while acknowledging equality of civil rights, and the egalitarian stream, emphasizing equality while preaching the liberty guaranteed by civil rights.

Liberal democracy understands rights as immunities from governmental interference. Their function is to prevent government from unduly restraining any individual's liberty. The egalitarian conception of rights is much broader than the classical liberal one and includes a wide range of positive benefits to be conferred by government. It tends toward an equality of results rather than merely of opportunities. To put it crudely, it means not only that you are free to apply for the job, but that you get it and you keep it.

Liberal democratic thought has as its economic counterpart the ideology of capitalism and a free-market economic system. The egalitarian stream issues in the ideology of socialism and a government dedicated to bringing about substantial economic equality among all citizens.

Liberalism as it exists in the United States today is an effort to have the best of both ideological worlds. It assigns to government the duty of fostering, not complete economic equality, but general prosperity and a more equal share in it for all citizens. At the same time, through an ever-expanding array of civil rights, it seeks to emancipate the individual from religious, moral, and social restraints that are not of his own choosing.

The contemporary liberal ideal would be a country in which everyone was employed at high wages in work which he/she found fulfilling, without distinction of race, color, creed, gender, ethnic origin, educational background, or sexual preference, and could live by any "lifestyle" that he/she chose.

Contemporary American conservatism is largely a reaction to this brand of liberalism, and therefore is a mixed bag of views. Among its adherents we find "conservatives" who are really nineteenth-century liberals eager to get government off the back of business. We also find "social-issue" conservatives angered by the liberal dissolution of our public morality. Still others are "libertarians" who want no public morality at all but oppose liberalism because of the large role it gives government. Another group of conservatives are regionalists or "states-righters" who are against, not government as such, but the Federal government.

The ideological conflict between and among liberals and conservatives is carried on in terms of liberty and equality. We all agree that all men are created equal and are endowed by their Creator with certain inalienable rights, among which are life, liberty, and the pursuit of happiness. Even if we leave the Creator out of the discussion—because He is "divisive" and so best not talked about in a pluralistic society—we still agree that we are equal and somehow endowed with inalienable rights.

Our political disputes consequently have a way of becoming arguments about rights. We operate in this country on what the late Alexander Bickel called a "liberal contractarian model" of society, which "rests on a vision of individual rights that have a clearly defined, independent existence predating society and are derived from nature and from a natural, if imagined, contract. Society must bend to these rights." All that is left to argue about is what the rights are, in the possession of which we are all equal. Clearly defined though the rights are assumed to be, we do not agree on what is included in them.

To that question there is no answer in terms of liberty and equality alone. Without some ordering principle that specifies the content of liberty and equality, we cannot harmonize the two goals. The ordering principle, to work effectively, must be outside of and above liberty and equality. It cannot be a vague "fraternity" but must be some commonly held judgment on what human beings are and what is truly good for them.

The mere thought of such a common moral principle superior to liberty and equality makes the contemporary liberal mind—and some conservative minds—shudder. We lack such an ordering principle because we are so devoted to liberty and equality as the supreme norms of a democratic society that we will not admit their subordination to any higher norms.

Yet liberty and equality cannot be the highest values of a political system because they relativize and ultimately destroy all other values. When we make them our supreme norms, we have no set of objectively valid human ends that can provide answers to the questions, liberty for what? and equality in what? We therefore cannot have the communal beliefs without which in the long run there is no community.

We have no firm basis on which such societal values as we happen to hold at a particular time can be transmitted from generation to generation. Even the most devout among us are prone to consider their moral convictions as merely private beliefs. Their children become unthinking moral relativists, as many a teacher today can testify.

In short, American society now lacks what Walter Lippmann called the public philosophy. We shall lack it increasingly as the moral and religious capital of our culture, on which liberalism has always traded even as it eroded it, is drained away. We are left with an unending battle between conflicting claims to liberty and equality, and no publicly acknowledged principle with which to resolve the conflict.

Lost in the Cosmos

If you want to know what is wrong with the Catholic Church, you read *The National Catholic Reporter*. You need go no farther. In fact, you really don't have to go that far. Almost any metropolitan daily or weekly newsmagazine has a number of disaffected Catholics on its staff who seldom miss a chance to point out the Church's deficiencies and defects.

One of them, not long ago, reporting on the exodus of young people from Ireland, remarked that it was not only the country's depressed economy that made them leave, but its repressive atmosphere. He quoted one young lady as saying that when the predominantly Catholic Irish people rejected a constitutional amendment to legalize divorce last year, she realized that she had had it with her native land. Not yet married, she could not abide the thought of not being able to get divorced. So brightly does the love of liberty burn in certain youthful hearts.

That the Church opposes liberty is the ordinary burden of the complaint against her. The liberty of which she unjustly deprives her suffering children usually turns out to be sexual freedom. The reason for the Church's harsh attitude, we are told, is a fear and hatred of sex that dates back to St. Augustine (or is it to St. Paul?), and prevents her from understanding modern men and women's healthy and guilt-free acceptance of their own sexuality.

But more interesting than what ex-Catholics reject is what the post-Christian world they have joined has to offer. Freedom to choose a lifestyle, yes, but beyond that, what? Well, success and money, of course; also devotion to approved progressive causes, and an interest in the arts. (Man does not live on sex alone.) But not much in the way of truth to believe in, or hope to live for, and none but human love to live on. Post-Christianity is mostly a negation.

It is intriguing to speculate on what makes negation so attractive to the modern mind. We must not underestimate the allurements of the world, the flesh, and the devil: they explain more than intellectual difficulties do. But there is a deeper reason, I believe, for contemporary loss of faith.

Part of it is a hatred of all authority, a hatred rooted in the modern ideal of the autonomous self. Modern man, formed by the liberal tradition, can see nothing in the exercise of authority but the imposition of one will on another.

John H. Hallowell, in his *The Decline of Liberalism as an Ideology*, says that liberalism in its original seventeenth-century form combined two elements: "first, the belief that society is composed of atomic, autonomous individuals; and, second, the belief that there are certain eternal truths transcending individuals and independent of either individual will or desire." Because they were confident that reason could recognize these transcendent truths, liberal societies were able to regard moral judgments and civil laws as exercises of reason and not merely as the imposition of the will of some people on others. But as liberal faith in reason's ability to rise above will and appetite waned, the liberal conception of society became that of a collection of individual wills guided at best by enlightened self-interest. Hence the hatred of authority, particularly ecclesiastical, but even of the authority of the democratic state.

Liberal societies today grant reason the ability to determine facts, discern patterns of causal relationship among facts, and figure out the most efficient means of achieving desired ends. Beyond that reason cannot go. Because it is saddled with this truncated conception of the scope of reason, the modern mind has an inborn dullness toward the very idea of transcendent truth. The notion of a truth beyond what meets the eye or is discovered by the scientific method is simply opaque to the typical mind of our age. Such a mind does not give a different answer from the Christian one to the question of the meaning and purpose of life; it does not even ask the question.

A number of sociologists have seen the roots of modern secularism in the industrialization of society, which applied to human work the purely instrumental conception of reason described above. Industrialism mechanizes work and "rationalizes" it by relentlessly pursuing the most efficient means of maximizing production while minimizing costs. The workers themselves become role-players in a mechanized process. Society as a whole is governed by bureaucracies which perform specified functions in accordance with impersonal rules. As Bryan R.

Wilson puts it in his *Religion in Sociological Perspective*:

> A modern social system is increasingly conceived as operating without virtues; it becomes a neutral, detached, objective, rational co-ordination of role performances. The system induces those who actually man the roles—that is, human beings—to behave as if they had neither virtues nor vices. The pressure is towards the neutralization of human personality so that roles might be performed with ever greater calculability.

We live, the sociologists tell us, in a world whose consciousness has been formed by these conceptions of man and his work. It is little wonder that the staple concerns of religion—good and evil, virtue and vice, the meaning and purpose of life—come to seem irrelevant in such a world—or that the human self now feels itself to be, as Walker Percy says, lost in the cosmos.

'*I hope its Ozone Friendly.*'

Why Anything Goes

One can say—if only for the sake of starting an argument—that liberal democracy in a pluralistic society is an endless but fruitless search for the lowest common denominator that can serve as society's moral bond. The more pluralistic the society, however, the more difficult it is to find a common denominator.

Let us try to explain the problem crudely and over-simply, but not entirely inaccurately. We did away with state churches in this country so that all Protestants could feel at home in it. We de-Protestantized the country so that Catholics, too, could feel at home in it. We have dechristianized the country to make Jews feel welcome, then dereligionized it so that atheists and agnostics may feel equally welcome. Now we are demoralizing the country so that deviants from accepted moral norms will not feel excluded. The lowest common denominator, we have discovered, is like the horizon, always approached but never reached.

As our consensus on basic principles of belief and morals evanesces, we fall back on shared material welfare as the sole social bond that it is both possible and necessary to maintain. We are a national community because we guarantee that no member of society will lack the minimal resources for living, but we leave the goals of life to individual judgment and choice. Freedom of choice in all matters that do not directly and seriously affect society's material welfare becomes society's highest ideal. As Justice Harry A. Blackmun put it in his dissenting opinion in the 1986 Georgia sodomy law case, "depriving individuals of their right to choose for themselves how to conduct their intimate relationships poses a far greater threat to the values most deeply rooted in our Nation's history than tolerance of nonconformity could ever do."

Contemporary liberalism thus manages to be at once both individualistic and statist. This ambivalence explains the otherwise puzzling spectacle of liberals who are simultaneously furiously indignant at anyone who is judged suspect of imposing his moral beliefs on others and grimly determined to use the agencies of the state to impose their vision of welfare on all the institutions of society. Their vision is of a religiously, spiritually, and morally neutral welfare state which confers its benefits equally on all the members of society without distinction of race, creed, age, sex, or sexual preference, and which prevents private institutions from making such distinctions either. Liberals will compel us to be free and equal—on their terms, not ours.

In criticizing this liberal conception of the welfare state, however, I do not reject the welfare state as such. I happen to think that George Will was right when he wrote in his *Statecraft as Soulcraft* that conservatism needs "an affirmative doctrine of the welfare state." The issue today is not whether we should have a welfare state, but what kind of welfare state, aiming at what goals and operating on what principles. The disease of contemporary liberal democracy is not its concern with the welfare of its citizens but the shallowness of its understanding of welfare.

Theodore J. Lowi, writing in the *Political Science Quarterly* (1986, no. 2), discusses this problem. "Liberalism," he says, "tries its best to take no position on the morality of conduct," and as a liberal himself he agrees that this is "the most reasonable approach to government in a pluralistic society." But he also argues that liberalism tends to make the ethic of the welfare state unworkable.

The older, pre-welfare state American ethic, he explains, had emphasized personal responsibility. The person who was primarily responsible for an injury (it could be either the injured but negligent employee or his negligent employer) was expected to bear the cost of the injury. If a person became dependent on the help of others, the question whether he himself had brought about his condition of dependency was considered highly relevant. The new welfare ethic replaced personal responsibility with a different principle: "All injuries and dependencies became part of the social system, and all costs related thereto became *social costs*," to be borne by society at large through a variety of insurance and entitlement programs.

Liberal refusal to make moral judgments, combined with the new welfare ethic, says Lowi, has put liberal government in a bind: "Once the new social ethic removed blame and replaced it with socialized responsibility, . . . everything became good to do, because all injuries and dependencies, regardless of source or cause, became 'social costs.'" Liberal government, he tells us, "has already become obliged to respond to any and every argument putting forward a case that a connection can be established between a particular conduct and some injurious consequence. This is why modern liberal government became a gigantic magnet of open-ended commitments without priorities."

Lowi urges liberals to face the problem they have created in the welfare state, because others are eager to do it for them by liquidating the welfare state. The solutions he suggests, however, remain purely technical and legal. They do not address the real problem, which is that the neutral state in a pluralistic society, having no moral priorities, can hardly avoid becoming "a gigantic magnet of open-ended commitments without priorities."

Papal Social Thought

When John Paul II's encyclical, *Sollicitudo Rei Socialis* (On Social Concern) appeared at the end of 1987, *The New Oxford Review* hailed it with delight as a socialist manifesto. More recently, in *Crisis*, Michael Novak has seen the encyclical as a belated papal discovery of what democratic capitalism has known all along, namely, the virtue of economic free enterprise. He quotes in evidence the passage (from section 15) of the encyclical:

> In today's world . . . *the right of economic initiative* is often suppressed. Yet it is a right which is important not only for the individual but also for the common good. Experience shows us that the denial of this right, or its limitation in the name of an alleged "equality" of everyone in society, diminishes, or in practice absolutely destroys the spirit of initiative, that is to say *the creative subjectivity of the citizen*. As a consequence, there arises, not so much a true equality as a "Leveling down." In the place of creative initiative there appears passivity, dependence and submission to the bureaucratic apparatus which, as the only "ordering" and "decision-making" body—if not also the "owner"—of the entire totality of goods and the means of production, puts everyone in a position of almost total dependence . . . similar to the traditional dependence of the worker-proletarian in capitalism.

But this is not quite so novel as Mr. Novak seems to think it is. In the line of "social encyclicals" that began with Leo XIII's *Rerum Novarum* in 1891 and has continued up to *Sollicitudo Rei Socialis*, there is a coherent tradition in which emphases vary but nothing is simply new. Thus, Leo XIII laid it down as a principle which "before all is to be considered as basic, namely, that private ownership must be preserved inviolate" (*RN*, no. 23). Seventy years later, in *Mater et Magistra* (no. 109), John XXIII reaffirmed that "the right of private property, including that pertaining to goods devoted to productive enterprises, is permanently valid" and "rooted in the very nature of things." The popes look upon private property as the spur to initiative and the source of wealth. "If incentives to ingenuity and skill in individual persons were to be abolished, the very fountains of wealth would necessarily dry up," said Leo XIII (*RN*, no. 22). Therefore, said Pius XI in *Quadragesimo Anno* (1931):

> Just as it is wrong to withdraw from the individual and commit to the community at large what private enterprise and industry can accomplish, so too, it is an injustice, a grave evil, and a disturbance of right order for a larger and higher organization to arrogate to itself functions which can be performed efficiently by small and lower bodies. This is a fundamental principle of social philosophy, unshaken and unchangeable, and it retains its full truth today. . . . the true aim of all social activity should be to help individual members of the social body, but never to destroy or absorb them.

Every succeeding pope has confirmed this principle, which has become known as the Principle of Subsidiarity.

One will look in vain in the encyclicals for a condemnation of capitalism, the free market, or competition simply as such. Pius XI said of capitalism that "the system itself is not to be condemned" and "is not vicious of its very nature," although it has been seriously abused. Similarly, he said, "free competition" is "within certain limits just and productive of good results." So, too, Paul VI, in no. 58 of *Popularum Progressio* (1967), acknowledged that free trade's "advantages are certainly evident when the parties involved are not affected by any excessive inequalities of power: it is an incentive to progress and a reward for effort."

What, then, were the popes criticizing in the severe language that they so frequently used about capitalism? Paul VI expressed the thought of all of them when he deplored (*PP*, no. 26) "a type of capitalism . . . which considers profit as the *key* motive for economic progress, competition as the *supreme* law of economics, and private ownership of the means of production as an *absolute* right that has no limits and carries no corresponding social obligation." I have italicized the words which explain why Paul VI, like his predecessors, described this system as "unchecked liberalism" and later said (no. 58) that "the rule of free trade, taken by itself, is no longer able to govern international relations," adding significantly that "one must recognize that it is the fundamental principle of liberalism, as the rule for commercial exchange, which is questioned here."

As the Principle of Subsidiarity indicates, the popes are fully aware that the energies of society well up from below in the initiative and enterprise of individuals and private associations. What they reject is the classical liberal faith in the unfailing efficacy of the market. Social order is not and cannot be the automatic product of market forces, or of Marxian laws of history, or of any other mechanically-functioning process. The just order which is the common good of society must be intended. It doesn't just happen if we set the autonomous individual free to pursue his own interest.

For that reason John Paul II can say (*SRS*, section 21) that both liberal capitalism and Marxist collectivism are "imperfect and in need of radical correction" (which, despite what some people have thought, is not to say that they are "morally equivalent"). He can also say (section 41) that the Church's social doctrine is not a "third way" between these two ideologies, because it is not itself an ideology but a moral theology which proposes the moral goals of human social life and the framework of moral principles within which men are to pursue those goals. The rest is politics, and "the church does not propose economic or political systems or programs, nor does she show preference for one or the other."

"Imposing" Moral Beliefs

New York's Archbishop, John Cardinal O'Connor, once wrote a pointed and pungent criticism of an unnamed public official for taking the waffling stand on the abortion issue which is now customary among certain Catholic politicians. This politician professed to have his own "deep reservations about abortion," but said, "I will not impose my own moral beliefs on others," apparently in the belief that abortion is a matter of purely private morality. The Cardinal commented that this was George Orwell's Newspeak, a species of doubletalk "deliberately constructed for political purposes."

As the Cardinal pointed out, this public official (like many another) "seems not to hesitate at all in 'imposing' his moral beliefs on others in regard to other highly contested public policy issues." It is only in regard to abortion (and certain other delicate subjects) that he develops scruples. Yet abortion raises the question of the worth of human life, and if that is not an issue of public policy, what is?

It does not cease to be a public issue because it is a moral issue. As another Catholic politician once remarked, "Of course you can legislate morality; there really isn't anything else to legislate." No one believes that more devoutly, most of the time, than the politicians who "refuse to impose their moral beliefs on others." Listen to their rhetoric and notice how often it is couched in terms of respect for rights, justice, charity, mercy, compassion, and other moral virtues.

Yet they use this moralistic language to justify public policy proposals which some people object to in equally moralistic terms as unjust and violative of *their* rights. There is no getting away from it: if justice is to be done at all, the morality of the larger and, we may hope, sounder part of the community will necessarily be imposed on some people who disagree with it. No culture can last if it concedes a veto power to every group in its midst that rejects the culture's norms.

Our American political culture, however, is in a fair way of granting that veto power in what are now called "social issues." This trend is particularly evident in the Democratic

Party. So, at any rate, political scientist Jo Freeman suggests in an article in the *Political Science Quarterly* (No. 3, 1986), in which she maintains that the Democratic and Republican parties have distinct political cultures.

The Republicans, she says, "have a unitary party in which great deference is paid to the leadership, activists are expected to be 'good soldiers,' and competing loyalties are frowned upon." Consequently, they conceive of representation on the model of "a trustee who pursues the long-range best interests of the represented."

To the Democrats, on the other hand, "representation does not mean the articulation of a single coherent program for the betterment of the nation but the inclusion of all relevant groups and viewpoints. Their concept of representation is delegatory, in which accurate reflection of the parts is necessary to the welfare of the whole." For this reason, she adds, "the party is very responsive to any groups, including such pariahs as gays and lesbians, that claim to be left out." I will add that this responsiveness gives homosexuals, feminists, pro-abortionists, and assorted minorities a veto on Democratic nominations. That veto power has more to do with the squeamishness of politicians about imposing their beliefs on others than any qualms of conscience do.

The Democratic Party historically has performed a necessary role, being the avenue through which groups ignored or rejected by the Republicans could make their way into the nation's public life. But the present structure of the party leaves the Democrats paralyzed by political dread where certain moral issues are involved. Dominated by their liberal wing, they are unable to admit that any standards are available for judging what makes for the moral health of the nation. To admit such standards, liberals allege, would deny the equality of all moral beliefs and would impose the beliefs of some on others.

But by rejecting the idea of moral truth and refusing to pass judgment on the validity of moral beliefs, liberals undermine democracy itself. What is the meaning of such basic democratic concepts as human rights or of such ringing phrases as the dignity of the human person, if we cannot allow ourselves to determine their content lest we impose the moral beliefs of some on others? More concretely, can we sustain the culture on which democracy depends if we refuse to decide such issues as the sanctity of life, elementary sexual morality, and the value of the stable monogamous family as the foundation of society?

Ideally, the democratic process is a serious and intelligent public debate on matters of public policy. (Yes, Virginia, we all know what it usually is in practice.) These are matters which inevitably involve issues of public morality. Because the process is democratic, all individuals and groups may take part in it. But because it concerns the *res publica*, the people's welfare, it arrives at public conclusions which at least in part are moral conclusions. The public cannot forever duck them on the ground that it does not want to impose its moral beliefs.

'It's just Moses name-dropping again.'

Civilization Is for the Civilized

Civilization depends on the civilized imposing their standards on the uncivilized. But who decides who the civilized are? The civilized do, that's who. If you can't accept that, you are against civilization.

Does that go down too hard? Then consider this: science is what scientists say it is. And who decides who are scientists? Scientists do. They set the standards by which persons are recognized as doing properly scientific work, as distinguished from dilettantism, quackery, and magic.

Doesn't this mean that science itself is only what a self-constituted elite chooses to accept as meeting its own arbitrarily determined standards? No, it does not. It certainly is open to that abuse. But to say that science is what scientists accept as science is only to say that science, like every branch of human knowledge, consists of the judgments arrived at by human minds striving to understand some aspect of the real world.

If there is no real world to understand, obviously there is no science. Neither is there any science if there are no minds capable of grasping and agreeing upon the structure of the real world. There is no set of facts "out there" which speaks to us and says, "We are science."

Science depends on minds that can judge what is a fact, which facts constitute evidence, and when the evidence leads to a firm conclusion. It also requires a community of persons who, however much they may disagree on any particular scientific question, recognize each other as possessing the training, the self-discipline, and the intellectual honesty needed to take part in the pursuit of scientific knowledge. Science must be in that sense self-validating, but it is not therefore arbitrary.

Something similar is true of every profession. Lawyers, doctors, accountants, professors, and journalists must develop and enforce the standards for the practice of law, medicine, accounting, university teaching, and journalism. It does not follow that each of these professions is a law unto itself; each of them is subject, when necessary, to regulation by the general community which it serves. Nonetheless, at least in the first instance, those engaged in each profession must develop the standards of the profession and must judge who are the persons qualified to practice it. There is no escaping the need for human judgment and, therefore, the necessity of relying on human minds.

That is all very well, you may say, when we are dealing with judgments about facts that can be verified or falsified by experience and are subject to empirical proof or disproof. In those cases, the real world as we experience it controls our judgments. But such is not the case when we make judgments about what is good or bad.

Those "value judgments," as positivists call them, are not judgments about the real world, but expressions of our feelings about the world, nothing more. For that reason, moral judgments are all subjective and relative. To see that this is so, we need only look at the enormous variety of moral standards that have obtained among the cultures and civilizations of mankind.

Before we cave in, however, and accept this standard argument for moral relativism, let us pause and ask ourselves how relative our judgments about human good and evil really are. Take, for the sake of discussion, the following two lists (for which I pretend neither completeness nor any great depth of philosophical analysis):

life	death
nourishment	starvation
health	sickness
material well-being	destitution
community	isolation
respect	humiliation
friendship	enmity
marriage	celibacy
family	childlessness
knowledge	ignorance
truth	error
meaning	meaninglessness

If we compare each item with the item directly opposite it, is there any doubt about which of them is good in itself and capable of being chosen for its own sake, and which of them is bad or at least not capable of being chosen for its own sake? Yes, yes, I know that people do sometimes commit suicide—but only because life has become bound up with pain, misery, or disgrace which they find intolerable, not because they do not recognize life as in itself good and death as the end of that good.

Monks and nuns renounce marriage, family and personal property, but only for the sake of a higher good, without which the renunciation would be senseless. No one pursues any of the items in the right hand column as ends in themselves. If someone does choose one or another of them, we ask what good he hopes to obtain by choosing something not choiceworthy in itself. We do not ask that question about people who choose life, health, friendship, marriage, knowledge, or truth.

What makes these things desirable is not merely the statistical fact that most people desire them, as if they could just as well desire the opposite. It is that these objects of choice answer to basic needs of human nature, without the satisfaction of which it cannot survive or flourish. The goods in the lefthand column can furnish a society with a list (a partial one, to be sure) of its goals. But a society which took the righthand column as its goals would be unendurable and would in fact not long endure. The civilized are those who are capable of understanding that.

Rights as the Beginning and End

I was paging through the *New York Times Book Review*, as is my wont of a Sunday afternoon, when my eye was caught by a brief, unsigned review of yet another book on abortion. According to the review, the author of the book concludes that, while the fetus has a right to life from the moment of conception, "this right to live does not entitle the fetus to use a woman's body against her will."

The issue, one notices, is posed in terms of rights and entitlements. "May I use your body, madam?" "Yes, dear, of course you may" or "No, you are not entitled to it and anyhow, I don't want you." Such language does not surprise us in a liberal society which thinks habitually in terms of rights. Yet even in a liberal society one must wonder by what tortuous mental process a man comes to discuss the morality of destroying human life as though he were a lawyer arguing a case of trespass on private property.

The fetus is cast as the party of the first part who pleads his right to live, which he cannot sustain without a temporary lease of the woman's body. She is the party of the second part who asserts an absolute property right to her own body. The court must decide which of these rights should prevail. Since the fetus, when all is said and done, is an intruder on someone else's property, he loses. That what he loses is his life may be regrettable, but the superior right has prevailed and so justice has been done.

But how does one come to think of the beginning of human life and the morality of ending it in these terms? The answer, I believe, is that one is an intellectual heir of John Locke and therefore thinks of a human being as essentially an individual proprietor.

In this view, each man is an island, of which he is the sole owner. He owns his body, the actions he performs with it, and the goods he acquires by those actions. In Locke's terminology, he is endowed by nature with original rights to life, liberty, and estate, which collectively form his "property." His only obligation is to respect the equal rights of other persons, all of whom are individual proprietors like himself.

Since disputes over rights inevitably arise, these proprietors enter into a social contract with each other, by which they form a civil society and set up a government with authority to resolve conflicts of rights. The contract into which individuals have freely entered obliges them to accept the government's decision in such cases.

But they remain what they were by nature: individuals distinct and separate from one another, each the owner of his own life, liberty, and estate. The relationship they have formed with one another by joining together in society is artificial, external, and contractual; it is not rooted in their nature as social beings. They formed the relationship so that each one could better protect his individual proprietary rights, and society's government has no function other than to protect those rights.

In the same spirit, the leaders of the French Revolution proclaimed in their Declaration of the Rights of Man and the Citizen that "ignorance, neglect, or contempt of the rights of men are the sole causes of public misfortunes and corruptions of Government." Implicit in this remarkable assertion is the proposition that if we only get our conception of rights straight and implement it in practice, we shall have solved all the problems of society and accomplished all the legitimate purposes of government.

This attitude prevails in influential circles in America today. Philosophers begin their political theories with the individual self and then seek to show how it can be incorporated into society without compromising its selfhood. Novelists depict and sometimes celebrate the war of the self against the restraints of society's culture. Newspapers and magazines, as the discerning reader will notice, often translate issues that affect all of society into struggles between conflicting rights.

Thus, for example, school busing becomes a conflict between the right of black parents to send their children to an integrated school and the right of white parents to send their children to a neighborhood school. Pornography is regarded, not as a social problem, but as a conflict between the right of some people to have access to "adult" material and the right of others not to have the same material thrown in their faces.

Even what to do about AIDS turns into a debate about rights.

The question, however, is not whether human beings have rights; they do, and few today will question that. Rather it is what model or picture of society should guide our thinking. In one model, which comes down to us from Aristotle and Aquinas, we think of man as a social being from whose nature flow relations to his family, neighbors, fellow-workers, the community, and the political order. These relations are the foundation of both rights and obligations which are prior to and independent of consent. In the Lockean model we conceive of man as an independent proprietor whose social relations are only those to which he has freely consented.

Individualists understandably prefer the second model, and the American Civil Liberties Union is hopelessly in love with it, but it leads to strange and distorted conclusions about social reality. If we take the principles of liberal individualism as axiomatic, we find it possible to think of the fetus and the woman as the parties of the first and second part arguing over their respective rights. We are then able to blind ourselves to the natural fact that they are related as mother and child and that the child is in the only natural place for him to be, his mother's womb.

Equal—and Separate

The dominant passion of a democratic society is the love of equality, said Alexis de Tocqueville in his classic *Democracy in America*, 150 years ago. In Strauss & Cropsey's *History of Political Philosophy*, Marvin Zetterbaum paraphrases Tocqueville in these words: "The characteristic feature of democratic society is its atomism. . . . Men confront each other as equals, each independent, each impotent. Individuals comprising such a society have, as citizens, no natural ties to one another; each being the equal of every other, no one is obliged to do the bidding of another." Equality means mutual independence limited only by contractual ties freely consented to.

Today, as the implications of this atomistic conception of equality relentlessly work themselves out, we must add that men and women confront each other as equals, each independent and bound by no natural ties. They are no longer the naturally complementary halves of the human race, but nearly identical and interchangeable units, united only by choice and for so long as the choice lasts.

As one might expect, those implications reveal themselves most clearly in that land of the future, Sweden. In an article distributed by the Swedish Information Service, an American sociologist, Linda Haas, describes Sweden's promotion of "equal parenthood." As the Swedish government reported to the United Nations, its sex-role policy was that "men were to be equally responsible for housework and childcare, while women were to be held equally accountable for the economic support of families." The premise of the policy is that men and women are equal in being identical in their roles in work and childcare.

In pursuit of this social goal, Swedish law provides for one year off from work, with pay, for either parent (or for both on an alternating part-time basis), to stay home and care for a newborn child. But men are not taking advantage of this opportunity in significant numbers, and most Swedish women do not want them to do so. According to a recent government report, says Haas, "only 27 per cent of all fathers whose wives were in the labor market before childbirth took even one day of parental leave for children born in 1982. Those who took leave took an average of only 49 days."

Among the reasons for this reluctance of men to take parental leave, Haas feels that "the most important may be attitudes toward the man as breadwinner. As long as men and women see men (rather than men *and* women) as responsible for the family's economic support, men's energies and interest will be directed toward occupational pursuits outside the home and away from childcare." Not only that, "women would have to be willing to give up their current freedom to choose whether or not to be employed outside the home." In fact, however, "women are still most comfortable with a situation where they are the ones primarily responsible for childcare" and they have "discouraged their partners from taking very much leave."

Changing such "deep-set" attitudes, Haas admits, "probably takes generations to accomplish." Nothing short of "a monumental resocialization effort" will suffice to reverse "traditional sex-role stereotyping." She seems to favor the effort, but she does not go on to consider the strong possibility that, should the effort succeed, it would increase the mutual independence of men and women, and further loosen the already weak ties that bind them together in Sweden.

Others, however, are willing to face the consequences of independence unflinchingly, to the point of renouncing marriage or even cohabitation altogether. One of them is Karen DeCrow, a former President of the National Organization for Women. She recently celebrated her 50th birthday by publishing a column in the New York *Times*, in which she said a number of sensible things about accepting one's age without trying to look younger than one really is. Then, determinedly unmarried though she is, she announced: "At 50, we learn that lust is underrated" and "leaves all other joys in the backfield."

That lust is underrated in this last quarter of the twentieth century came as a surprise to me. But DeCrow speaks from experience, and I do not, so I can't argue with her. I can't help wondering, however, if she fully appreciates the significance of her own remark, "At 50, time is on fast-forward."

At 50, one would think, a woman finds it harder to attract

desirable sex partners than she did at 25. At 55, it will be harder still, and at 60, still harder again. A woman who wants to keep up an active sex life through her fifties and sixties may discover that she needs one steady, reliable, and devoted partner; in short, a husband. But Ms. DeCrow will have none of that.

"Perfect love," she says, is possible, but only "if one does not give up one's name or personal finances or place to live." Perfect love, it appears, asks only: Your place or mine? Nor need it ask any other question if one identifies love with the joy that leaves all others in the backfield. Evidently DeCrow agrees with Eliza Doolittle's father in *My Fair Lady*: "You can 'ave it all and not get 'ooked."

Or, as Fred Astaire sang in one of his films, "It's nice work if you can get it." But can you get it just by trying hard enough? For the definitive answer to that question, we may have to await another report from Karen DeCrow when she turns 60.

Stooping to Folly

Two hundred and more years ago, in what must seem to us a vanished Age of Innocence, Oliver Goldsmith wrote:

When lovely woman stoops to folly,
And finds too late that men betray,
What charm can soothe her melancholy?
What art can wash her guilt away?

No poet could write that verse today, for lovely woman no longer stoops to folly. Or rather, she does, but she doesn't know it's folly and she doesn't know she stoops. A true child of her time, she is simply "sexually active" and unaware of sin, or guilt, or shame. Neither does she see any inherent meaning or significance in what she does. She is an emancipated woman, committed to nothing but the satisfaction of her own needs.

She and her boyfriend have learned to think for themselves, which is no strain on their brains, however, since what they really want is freedom to decide for themselves, and they can do that either with more thought or less. If they are in a hurry, they make do with less.

In the nineteenth century it was still possible for John Stuart Mill to advocate maximum freedom for the individual as the source of society's intellectual and moral progress. Mill recommended "the fullest liberty of professing and discussing, as a matter of ethical conviction, any doctrine, however immoral it may be considered." But he proposed this liberty of discussion in the belief that unlimited discussion would lead society at large to a fuller grasp of the truth. "As mankind improves," he said, "the number of doctrines which are no longer disputed or doubted will constantly be on the increase" and there will be "a consolidation . . . of true opinions" and "a gradual narrowing of the bounds of diversity of opinion."

Similarly, he argued, society needs exceptional and unconventional persons "to commence new practices and set the example of more enlightened conduct and better taste and sense in human life." Shocking as society may at first find these persons' "experiments" in living, if the experiments prove successful, they will elevate society's manners and morals and society will make progress.

I have several times taught a course on Mill's essay, *On Liberty*, from which the above quotations are taken. Toward the end of the course I have asked a question: Now that society has so largely accepted Mill's doctrine and established the freedom of speech and conduct that he advocated, have we achieved the results that he promised? Do we find in our society a growing agreement on truth and a steady elevation of the standards of taste and conduct?

The students' response is to look at me as if I had just come in from outer space and were asking the way to the next galaxy. They cannot imagine why freedom should have any connection with truth or morality. What difference does it make whether our intellectual and moral standards have gone up or down? What indeed can "up" and "down" mean in relation to such highly subjective concepts as truth and moral good? We are free for the sake of being free, not because freedom will make us wiser and better.

When I see the students' puzzled looks, I realize once again how hopelessly out of date both John Stuart Mill and I are (each, of course, in his own very different way). Contemporary society does not believe in a common human nature or in any other objective standard by which we may judge up and down, true or false, better and worse. It believes only in what a writer in *Time* once called "the new secular religion of the self."

Like most things new, this secular religion has roots far in the past. As Hannah Arendt explained in *The Human Condition*, "One of the most persistent trends in modern philosophy since Descartes and perhaps its most original contribution to philosophy has been an exclusive concern with the self, as distinguished from the soul or person or man in general, an attempt to reduce all experiences, with the world as well as with other human beings, to experiences between man and himself."

"All men are created equal" thus becomes the proposition that all selves are equal precisely in their quality of being selves. Much of contemporary liberal political theory is based on the primacy of the self. The self, to John Rawls in *A Theory of Justice*, is prior to the ends that it affirms. Human life has no natural or God-given purposes, but only those which the self chooses for itself. Therefore, as Ronald Dworkin says in his essay, *Liberalism*, "government must be neutral on what might be called the question of the good life." The conservative critic, George Will, makes the same point in his *Statecraft as Soulcraft*: "The fundamental goal of modern liberalism has been equality, and it has given us government that believes in the moral equality of appetites."

Liberal individualism leads also to what John Zvesper has called "the reduction of education to urbane, enlightened skepticism." If all values are individual and subjective, they are all relative, and all that education can do for us is to show us that. There is a further consequence, which Thomas Spragens points out in *The Irony of Liberal Reason*: "Since all the dogmatic relativist can conceive is individual interests anyway, he would be unable to see or describe a process of cultural disintegration if it unfolded before his very eyes." And that, dear reader, is why lovely woman nowadays stoops to folly without being able to see what she is doing.

The Problem of Evil

Cardinal Ratzinger has remarked that the problem of evil has exercised the minds of men at least since the *Book of Job*. That book, however, has not succeeded in putting everyone's mind at rest on the question of why God permits evil to afflict the just as well as the unjust. I remember a lunch-table conversation some years ago in which a young priest said that he had never found God's answer to Job satisfactory. I understood how he felt, but I suspect that it is the only answer we shall ever get, because it is the only answer we can get.

You will recall that after Job's long lament about his afflictions and his friends' efforts to be helpful by assuring him that his sufferings must be the penalty for his sins, God scolds the friends for their presumption, then directs a lengthy speech to Job. Briefly and colloquially put, God's answer to Job comes down to this: "Were you there when I made the world? You weren't? Then shut up!"

And rightly. It would be impossible for the Lord who brought the universe into being out of nothing to get finite minds to see the situation as it was, so to speak, on the day before the creation, when all the options were open. Nor could He enable us to understand why He chose to create this world rather than another and possible one. *Omnia exeunt in mysterium*: at the end of every line of inquiry, the human mind encounters mystery.

We must therefore accept what we cannot possibly comprehend. We must also admit that we have no standards by which we can find God or His universe wanting, because we could get such standards only from the universe that God made. To what are we appealing when we declare the heavens unjust? Beyond the universe as it is, there is only God, and beyond God there is nothing. There is no standard above Him by which we can pass judgment on Him or His works.

One thought, however, occurs to me, not as solving the problem of evil, but as perhaps throwing some light on it. It is that most of the evil in the world is the result of God's having decided to create free creatures. When we think of evil, we think too readily of the loss of life, the suffering, and the damage caused by earthquakes, hurricanes, plagues, and other natural disasters—what insurance companies call acts of God. But the worst horrors of our world, from the crimes of Hitler, Stalin, Mao, Pol Pot, and Idi Amin to the daily diet of tales of cruelty, exploitation, and degradation served up in each morning's newspaper, are not natural disasters or "acts of God." Directly or indirectly, they are due to human beings choosing evil.

We could, and some of us do, blame God for having made us free, but that is tantamount to blaming Him for having made us at all. It is our nature to be free, and without our freedom, we would not be human. Our freedom makes our crimes and sins possible, but it is also what makes us, as the Bible says, the image and likeness of God, capable of freely serving Him, capable also of sharing in His divine life forever.

To live as a human being is to choose. Life is choice, a destiny from which we cannot escape by refusing to choose, and the necessity of choice entails the possibility of choosing evil as well as good. From this possibility God will not save us by depriving us of our freedom, for in so doing He would dehumanize us. We are His creatures, but His free creatures, and He will not save us against our wills.

The consequences of the human abuse of freedom are horrendous, and they explain most of the evils from which mankind suffers. We could cope with a world in which the only disasters were natural ones. It is pride, greed, lust, anger, envy, gluttony, and sloth that cause the evils which we inflict on one another and so often make human life a hell.

The consequences of sin fall upon the innocent as well as the guilty, often from generation to generation. Among these consequences is a genuine lessening and diminution of freedom, not all of it due to our personal sins. None of us today enjoys a godlike freedom which easily and without struggle resists temptation. We have inherited a nature which is free indeed, but weakened and blinded by the sins of our ancestors, right back to the first ones, and which is therefore prone to repeat and multiply the sins of the past.

It is this fallen and sinful world into which Christ came

to save us. He does not do it by taking us out of this world; our salvation is accomplished here, in the world as it is. Nor does He restore the lost paradise or promise a future one to be built by reforming social institutions. Above all, He does not save us by taking away the freedom that makes sin possible, or by abolishing sin's dreadful consequences. His salvation takes place within each of us individually, through the grace that heals our wounded wills and enables us to grow into a life lived without sin and in harmony with God's will.

I do not mean to imply that social institutions do not need to be reformed—how could the institutions of proud, greedy, and lustful men not need reform?—or that reforming them would do no good. But, as every papal encyclical on social questions insists, no reform will work without a profound conversion of our wills from evil to good. The "problem of evil" lies mainly in our freedom and what we have done with it. The mystery remains: why God in His infinite wisdom chose to create and then redeem the likes of us.

'Forgive us our alleged trespasses.'

Christian Freedom

Christians though we claim to be, today we dislike the notion of sin, with its connotation of personal responsibility and guilt. If we speak of sin at all, it is not personal sin but social sin, the kind we can wash away by changing institutions without changing ourselves.

Granted, there are unjust social structures which people cling to because of their personal pride and greed, not to mention envy and sloth. As the popes have insisted with increasing frequency in the last hundred years, these structures will not be changed for the better unless multitudes of individuals are willing to reshape their personal attitudes and habits. But blaming the system rather than ourselves remains a tempting cop-out, and many there are who resort to it. Modern men are appalled at the idea that God holds them responsible for what they do and might actually punish them for it. Some of them, including nominal Christians, refuse to believe in a God who could treat them in that way.

Yet if we mean to be Christians, we must recognize that the New Testament takes sin very seriously. The mission of Christ was one of redemption, but of redemption precisely from sin. Jesus, as the New Testament presents Him, came to save us from the consequences of our sins, both original and personal, and His life and death make no sense except in that light. If sin means nothing, neither does salvation; we do not need to be saved from a ship that isn't sinking.

According to the New Testament, however, the ship is sinking: "Unless you repent, you will all likewise perish" (Lk 13:3). "Repent, for the kingdom of heaven is at hand," cried John the Baptist (Mt 3:2). When John was arrested and imprisoned, Jesus took up the same theme and "began to preach, saying, 'Repent, for the kingdom of heaven is at hand'" (Mt 4:17).

Jesus passed a severe judgment on those whom His preaching and miracles did not lead to repentance: "The men of Nineveh will arise at the judgment with this generation and condemn it, for they repented at the preaching of Jonah, and behold, something greater than Jonah is here" (Lk 11:32). "It shall be more tolerable on the day of judgment for Tyre and Sidon, and for the land of Sodom, than for you" (Mt 11:22,24).

For there will be a day of judgment. At the end of this world, Jesus will come to judge us all. To the saved He will say: "Come, O blessed of my Father, inherit the kingdom prepared for you from the foundation of the world." To the damned He will say: "Depart from me, you cursed, into the eternal fire prepared for the devil and his angels. . . . And they will go away into eternal punishment, but the righteous into eternal life" (Mt 25:34,41,46). "And this," says St. John, "is the judgment, that the light has come into the world, and men loved darkness rather than light, because their deeds were evil" (Jn 3:19).

Sin, therefore, is to be dreaded above every other evil: "If your hand causes you to sin, cut it off. . . . And if your foot causes you to sin, cut it off. . . . And if your eye causes you to sin, pluck it out; it is better for you to enter the kingdom of God with one eye than with two eyes to be thrown into hell, where the worm does not die, and the fire is not quenched" (Mk 9:43,45,47).

This is tough talk: hard and utterly uncompromising. It is not the only talk we hear from the lips of Jesus; the parable of the Prodigal Son is as much a part of the New Testament as is the Last Judgment. But there is no denying that the tough talk is there and is basic to the message that the New Testament conveys to us, which is that God became man to save us from our sins, not from our weaknesses and mistakes.

Frightening though we may find the idea of inescapable divine judgment to be, we ought to admit that God really pays us a compliment by treating us as sinners who can repent rather than as automatons which cannot help what they do, or as immature children who are not responsible for what they do, or as victims of our passions who are more to be pitied than censured. Any or all of the above may at times be true of us because we are creatures and are not endowed with complete and divine mastery over ourselves (a fact of which God surely is at least as well aware as we are). But it is the glory of our nature that we are free creatures, made in the image and likeness of God inasmuch as we are endowed with intelligence and the power of free and rational choice.

It is as such that Our Lord takes us.

One of the most striking features of the New Testament is that Jesus speaks to very ordinary, undistinguished human beings as to responsible adults who are accountable for their own actions. He honors the humblest of them by respecting their humanity and acknowledging that, much as we all need and depend on God's help (without which, He tells us, we can do nothing), their ultimate and eternal destiny is in their own hands. God's judgment on us registers what we have chosen to make of ourselves.

Four and a half centuries ago, St. Angela Merici, the foundress of the Ursuline nuns, beautifully expressed this Christian appreciation of human freedom. In her spiritual testament, she urged her nuns to treat the girls they taught with firm but loving kindness, so that the instructions they gave them should not seem to be imposed by force. "For God," she said, "has given everyone liberty, and therefore He compels no one, but only points the way, calls, and persuades." God has more respect for our freedom than we often have ourselves.

Going to Hell

On the Last Day, when the living and the dead are judged, they will not be judged by me. You find that a consoling thought, I'm sure. So do I, because I don't feel up to passing the final judgment on anyone, let alone the whole human race.

Nevertheless, the human race will be judged. Each of us must hear from the lips of Him who can pronounce them the words, "Come, you blessed of my Father, inherit the kingdom prepared for you from the foundation of the world," or "Depart from me, you cursed, into the eternal fire prepared for the devil and his angels." We have it from the Lord himself that the latter "will go away into eternal punishment, but the righteous into eternal life."

Now, however, we have it from Professor Martin E. Marty, a church historian at the University of Chicago, that the idea of eternal punishment in hell is not "culturally available." That is to say, we can no longer appeal to the fear of hell to get people to do anything or to abstain from anything, because almost no one really believes in hell anymore.

There is no denying that what Professor Marty says is true of an indeterminate but surely large number of people today. But it is curious that it should be true in a society in which most people profess to be theists and even Christians.

It is not strange, of course, that those who do not believe in God do not believe in hell, either. (There are others who do believe in God but not in the immortality of the soul or the resurrection of the body. Life in this world, they hold, is God's gift but it is His only gift and when it ends, we cease totally to be.) What is strange is that those who hope, however vaguely, for eternal life with God would take it as a given with no alternative.

Human beings are good enough at creating hells on earth that it should occur to them as a distinct possibility that they may be headed for something similar in life after death. Lenin, Stalin, Mao, Fidel Castro, and Pol Pot may sincerely have intended to bring about heaven on earth, but in fact they produced the opposite. The small-scale but brutal criminals about whom we read every day in the newspapers have not turned New York, Chicago, or Los Angeles into the earthly paradise. Others—active alcoholics, drug addicts, men and women enslaved to compulsive sex drives—may be more to be pitied than censured, but they make life a hell for themselves and others while they are here.

Nothing in our experience in this world assures us that all stories must have happy endings. No empirical evidence gives us ground for believing that, if there is life after death, we are bound to live it in heaven. The evidence that meets our eyes suggests the contrary.

We have an understandable resistance to the idea of an eternity in hell, but our repugnance for it is sentimental rather than intellectual. "To understand everything is to forgive everything" is a famous phrase but, as George Bernard Shaw commented, it is the devil's sentimentality. Human wickedness is real, God knows—and we know it too.

But, we feel, nothing that a human being can do is so wicked as to merit punishment forever, and a good God would not inflict it. This objection, however, assumes that we are born saved and do not need to achieve salvation. But we are not born saved; the Bible tells us that we are born in sin. Leaving aside the doctrine of original sin, it is clear that we are born immature. Small children are enormously appealing but they are also enormously demanding and self-centered. If they do not develop past that stage as they grow up, they turn out to be monsters. Even in purely this-worldly terms, we all need salvation from our innate selfishness, and it is not guaranteed in advance. It is a mistake to think that God could have created us in heaven, with salvation already achieved, and that it was hardhearted of Him to make us pass a test to get what He could have given us gratis in the first place. It is a child's view of life to look upon all standards of performance as imposed on us from without by Mommy, Daddy, teacher, the parish priest, the cop on the corner and, behind them all, that Supercop, God. The standards of performance are given to us from within by our nature as human beings.

We are indeed creatures who have nothing that God did not give us. But we are free creatures endowed with intelligence and the power of choice. President John F. Kennedy was fond of the French aphorism, *gouverner, c'est choisir*—to govern is to choose. More generally, to live a human life is to choose. God's grace gives us the inspiration and the power to choose the good, but God cannot choose for us. He only makes the final and infallible judgment on what we have freely made of ourselves.

"We must picture Hell," says C.S. Lewis in *The Screwtape Letters*, "as a state . . . where everyone has a grievance, and where everyone lives the deadly serious passions of envy, self-importance, and resentment." Such persons are in hell because they have made themselves incapable of heaven. As a seventeenth-century Archbishop of Canterbury explained, "The pleasures of Heaven itself could signify no good or happiness to that man who is not so disposed as to take pleasure in them."

Culturally available or not, the thought that we determine our eternal destiny for good or ill is worth reflecting on in this Easter season. We shall rejoice the more in the Resurrection as the pledge of our salvation if we understand clearly what we are saved from and how much we need a Savior from it.

A Disintegrating Culture

The American Catholic scene at the present time is populated by Catholics, semi-Catholics, semi-demi-Catholics, communal Catholics and, of course, ex-Catholics. There are also, we have lately been informed, Core Catholics, said to be the heart and soul of the American Church, who follow Church teaching when they agree with it and reject it when they do not. It is highly dubious whether a church that accomodates itself to that scene has a future.

The percentages of Catholics, semi-Catholics, etc., may not be accurately reported by the sociologists, pollsters, and journalists, but that is not the question of primary importance. Even if there are more Catholics of the orthodox persuasion than these reporters would have us believe, there is no denying that hosts of American Catholics, both clerical and lay, are more or less typical products of the culture in which they live, and to that extent are semi-Catholics at best.

That is simply a fact which any teacher in a Catholic school encounters almost daily. To cite but one example out of my own experience, not long ago I asked a young woman in one of my classes what she thought of laws which New Jersey and Alabama had passed denying welfare benefits to unmarried but cohabiting parents of children, and which the U.S. Supreme Court had declared unconstitutional as denying the equal protection of the laws to the illegitimate children. She began her reply by saying, "Well, of course, raised as I have been raised, I wouldn't consider having a child out of wedlock, but other people have been raised differently, and for them it might not be wrong." It was, alas, an all too typical student response.

I have no doubts about this young lady's virtue, for she is very much a lady. But her unwillingness to say that something was wrong in itself and not merely for her personally showed that she was, as Mr. Springsteen puts it, born in the U.S.A., a product of our liberal and disintegrating culture.

That culture, insofar as it is shaped by liberalism, is a blend of libertarianism and egalitarianism. As libertarian, it proclaims every individual's right to choose his own "values" and standards of belief and conduct. It thereby weakens people's moral convictions by teaching them that their beliefs have no objective validity and are only statements of personal choice. At the same time it bolsters their faith in their right to do whatever seems best to them. On the other hand, as egalitarian, it calls in the power of the state to impose libertarianism on all the institutions of society, private as well as public.

One of the more extreme examples of this coercive egalitarianism is the District of Columbia's Human Rights Act, under which Georgetown University has been obliged to grant to homosexual student organizations the same access to university facilities and funds as other student organizations. This Act forbids any educational institution in the District to discriminate in affording access to its facilities and services on grounds of "race, color, religion, national origin, sex, age, marital status, personal appearance, sexual orientation, family responsibilities, political affiliation, source of income, or physical handicap."

The statute reads like a list of the only offenses that the modern mind regards as sins: racism, sexism, ageism, the various "isms" of religious and ethnic prejudice, "homophobia," bias against extramarital cohabitation, and what, for want of a better word, I will call anti-slobbism. But since it is a statute and as such has the force of law, it uses the power of government, in the name of equality, to deprive private institutions of the freedom to define their own standards in religion, morals, or even manners.

This is not a matter of merely local interest in the District of Columbia. In February, 1988, Jeff Levi, Executive Director of the National Gay and Lesbian Task Force, sent out an "action alert" in which he announced that a homosexual civil rights bill was pending in Congress and that "every Democratic candidate for the presidency has pledged to sign that bill into law" (the Republicans prudently refused to answer him). Should such a bill become law, its legal effect would be that once again equality would override the freedom of private institutions. Its more significant cultural effect would be to impress it more deeply on the public mind that all sexual preferences are only that—preferences and, as such, equal. The flattening-out of our culture and its reduction to an ever-sinking lowest common denominator would reach a new depth.

The important question facing the Catholic Church in this country, its hierarchy in particular, is whether the Church can survive by adapting its teaching to this culture. It is not whether the Church can survive in a democracy; it has long since proved that it can not only survive but flourish. The issue rather is whether the Church can keep itself alive by accomodating itself to the opinions and desires of a membership increasingly infected by a soft, relativistic egalitarianism.

One understands the pastoral urge of bishops, priests, and theologians to "speak to all our people" and to drive no one out of the Church. But the consequences of making that urge the basis of pastoral policy and of trying to satisfy unending complaints about discrimination are likely to be ruinous. One need only look at the experience of the liberal Protestant denominations to see what trying to keep up with the times leads to.

Those Who Care, Govern

Those who don't care are governed by those who do care. Theoretically, in a democracy the majority governs, or at least chooses the officials who govern, and in this way the majority shapes public policy. In practice, however, the moving and shaping forces of politics frequently are activist minorities.

It is probably inherent in the nature of a mass democracy that this should be so. If we want democracy, we want the key posts in government to be filled by election. Therefore, we want public officials who aspire to be elected or re-elected. In order to get elected, they must calculate how many votes they stand to win or lose by what they do. That calculation will often enough lead them to act in ways that have little to do with the public good or the wishes of a majority.

For example, I recall the time when I first heard it proposed to lower the voting age to 18. There was no massive demand for this change but, as I wrote at the time, it was a proposal that could not fail to be adopted. No politician who opposed it would win votes, but he could and would lose some votes. The great majority (including the young) that had no strong feelings about the matter would not thank him for being against lowering the voting age, but the minority that wanted the change would remember at the next election and punish him.

So the proposal to lower the voting age to 18 went through and became the 26th Amendment to the Constitution. There is little reason to believe that the republic is better governed as a result or that its supposed beneficiaries are particularly pleased with the benefit conferred on them. The 18-21 age group is even more apathetic than the rest of the electorate in exercising the right to vote.

This example illustrates a more general truth which Robert A. Dahl enunciated in his *A Preface to Democratic Theory*: "The making of governmental decisions is not a majestic march of great majorities united upon certain matters of basic policy. It is the steady appeasement of relatively small groups." That is a pretty accurate description of the way in which our pluralistic mass democratic system actually works, and it throws light on some otherwise strange results that the system produces.

The Civil Rights Restoration Act of 1988, for instance. This act of Congress had its origin in a case involving Grove City College, a small liberal-arts institution in Pennsylvania. The college on principle had accepted no federal funds because it did not want to be subject to federal regulations. Nonetheless, because some of its students had federally-backed loans, stipends, or grants, it "became entangled," in the words of the New York *Times*, "in a legal battle with the Government when it separated boys and girls in the school's intramural sports program and refused to file a statement of compliance with Title IX of the 1972 Education act, which bars discrimination on the basis of sex."

The case was carried up to the U.S. Supreme Court, which held in 1984 that the college was indeed bound by Title IX, but only in that part of its operations which was affected by the student loans and grants, namely, its admissions office. This decision enraged the civil-rights activists but seemingly made little impression on the rest of the population.

After four years of lobbying by civil-rights groups, Congress passed the Civil Rights Restoration Act. It subjects to federal regulation every aspect of the operations, not only of schools, but of all private institutions that directly or indirectly receive federal funds. President Reagan vetoed this act, but Congress repassed it over his veto, and it is now the law of the land.

Why did Congress do this? *Time* explained that, despite last-minute efforts by conservative Protestant groups to persuade Congress not to override the President's veto, "even most Republicans seemed less impressed by the evangelical broadsides than by the dangers of voting against anything called a civil-rights act in an election year." As for the Democratic Party, it is gripped in a stranglehold by the "rainbow coalition" to which Garry Wills has ascribed the defeat of Robert Bork's appointment to the Supreme Court: "minorities, women's groups, civil liberties activists." One cannot imagine the Democrats drawing the wrath of these groups down upon themselves in an election year or any other year.

There is a similar explanation for what the New York *Times* headlined as "A Gay Rights Victory at Georgetown." In an action brought under the District of Columbia's Human Rights Act, the District's Court of Appeals forced Georgetown University to give homosexual students the same privileges as other student groups, despite the university's argument that it would violate the school's Catholic principles and deprive it of its religious freedom. The only concession the homosexual students had to make was an agreement to print on their literature a notice that their views "are not endorsed by Georgetown University."

Georgetown's president has understandably tried to put the best face he can on his defeat by pointing out that the university was not obliged to give the homosexuals "official recognition." But, as he says himself, "the holding of the court is clear: The District of Columbia has a compelling interest in eradicating discrimination against homosexuals, and that overrides the First Amendment protection of Georgetown's religious objections to subsidizing homosexual organizations."

Where does the District of Columbia get this "compelling interest"? Surely not from the "majestic march of great majorities," but from "the steady appeasement of relatively small groups." That's democracy: those who care govern those who don't.

Ordered Liberty

I once read somewhere that the trouble with liberals is that they have not yet noticed the twentieth century. That is still true of by far the greater number of them. But as our century staggers to its close, some of them are beginning to take note of it.

The New Republic, for instance, which is certifiably liberal, remarked in an editorial on February 8, 1988 on liberal blindness to "cultural decline." Liberals, it said, do not want to see this unpleasant reality because it "challenges their own attachment to the endlessness of personal freedoms. . . . Contemporary liberalism is so intellectually and psychologically invested in the doctrine of ever-expanding rights—the rights of privacy, the rights of children, the rights of criminals, the rights of pornographers, the rights of everyone to everything—that any suggestion of the baleful consequences of that doctrine appears to them as a threat to the liberal idea itself."

Whether it is a threat depends on what one thinks is "the liberal idea itself." Liberalism as a theory of ethics and politics lasted as long as it did and worked as well as it did because it assumed that rational and decent people would see the difference between moral right and wrong and would for the most part respect it. Liberalism, however, was able to do this because it incorporated into its idea of personal freedom moral norms which it did not create but inherited from the classical and Christian past.

As liberals have used up this moral capital, they have come to regard these or any other transcendent moral norms as threats to the liberal idea itself. They may well be right, too, because the core of liberalism has always been the autonomy of the individual and his right to decide for himself which norms he will obey.

Those who think that today's liberals are wrong—as *The New Republic* does when it proposes "the subtle truth that it really is wise restraints that make us genuinely free"—will have to revise the liberal idea of freedom. Above all, they will have to remove from the core of liberalism the belief that liberty consists in the sovereignty of the individual and his indefeasible right to decide for himself. More than two hundred years ago Edmund Burke put the key question: "Even in matters which are, as it were, just within our reach, what would become of the world, if the practice of all moral duties, and the foundations of society, rested upon having their reasons made clear and demonstrative to every individual?"

A sounder idea of freedom is contained in the phrase, ordered liberty, of which the U.S. Supreme Court has become fond. Despite the bizarre implications the Court has found in it (abortion on demand, for example), the phrase in itself is a good one and, properly used, could provide an antidote to the corrosive acid of individualism.

To quote Burke once again (he was speaking of the British constitution, but his words will apply to our own as well): "The distinguishing part of our constitution is its liberty. . . . But the liberty, the only liberty I mean, is a liberty connected with order; that not only exists along with order and virtue, but which cannot exist at all without them."

The order without which liberty cannot exist has several levels. It is a legal and political order, a social order, and a cultural order constituted by commonly-held conventions, codes of manners, moral principles, and beliefs about the nature of man and his place in the world. At its deepest level, it rests on belief in divine revelation, or on the conviction that the order of creation is open and accessible to human reason, or on both together. Ordered liberty depends upon an ordered universe.

It cannot be produced by a merely fabricating reason which tries to construct its own order out of its desires. Ordered liberty must be based on principles outside of and higher than our wishes, as Burke explained: "Men are qualified for civil liberty in exact proportion to their disposition to put moral chains upon their own appetites. . . . Society cannot exist unless a controlling power upon will and appetite be placed somewhere, and the less of it there is within, the more there must be without. It is ordained in the eternal constitution of things that men of intemperate mind cannot be free. Their passions forge their fetters."

It is the nature of our freedom that, if we abuse it, we lose it. This result is obvious in the case of persons who become enslaved to alcohol, drugs, gambling, or other addictions. But the pride, greed, lust, anger, envy, gluttony, and sloth with which we are all infected also forge fetters which are no less fetters for being called rights. Hence our need for "wise restraints that genuinely make us free," and the further need to recognize an overarching moral order from which we may learn what restraints are truly wise.

This idea will not sit well with liberals who believe in "the rights of everyone to everything." As Burke said of their French revolutionary forebears, "The little catechism of the rights of men is soon learned, and the inferences are in the passions." But if neither reason nor revelation is permitted to furnish us with standards by which to distinguish spurious from valid claims to rights, all such claims must be mere assertions of the individual's passionate desires.

This conclusion, however, leads to the attempt, characteristic of contemporary liberalism, to found the order of law and politics on equal respect for the passions of all individuals. George Sabine, an historian of political thought, has described what lies at the end of that road: "The absolutely sovereign and omnicompetent state is the logical correlate of a society which consists of atomic individuals." Such a state need not be a brutal dictatorship. It could be a soft bureaucratic despotism operating on the principles of the American Civil Liberties Union.

Plastic People

Dustin Hoffman first achieved fame as an actor with the role of Benjamin in *The Graduate*. You may recall that the film opens with a party given in honor of Benjamin's graduation from college. One of the men present puts his arm around him and says: "Benjamin, I have only one word to say to you: plastics." That scene has remained in my memory ever since as a perfect parable for our times and a paradigm of the modern mind.

Plastics are artificial substances made by breaking down natural substances into their component elements, and then reconstituting them in forms not produced by natural processes. All that nature contributes to the final product is its constituent elements; the product's form and structure are the work of man. Plastics, therefore, are another stride forward in man's conquest of nature, by which he bends it to his will. Modern man is the analyzer and synthesizer who breaks the world into bits and reshapes it to serve his purposes.

Plastics, moreover, are not just the stuff of which we make shopping bags and guns that can be smuggled past metal detectors into airports. We are increasingly able to treat living organic material as plastic, capable of being remolded to suit our designs. Much has already been done in that direction with brute animals. The new frontier is the manipulation of human genetic material.

Prof. Lee M. Silver of Princeton University presented a statement to a subcommittee of Congress on July 14, 1988, in which he described some of the things we shall be able to do with human genetic material when the technology we now use on other animals has been sufficiently improved to be used on human beings. He saw four areas in which "advances in human reproductive technology could occur."

The first was a "drastic" increase in the success rate of *in vitro* fertilization and embryo freezing. As we all know, some "test-tube" babies have already been born who were conceived *in vitro*, i.e., in glass, outside the womb and later implanted in their mothers' bodies. But the survival rate of such transferred embryos is low. With further research, however, *in vitro* fertilization might become "a routine medical procedure accessible to the general population."

If embryo freezing (freezing an embryo conceived in glass for further use) should also become a routine procedure, a woman could freeze now, get pregnant later. Or she could have a batch of her ova fertilized, then frozen to thaw out and use if her first attempts at transferring embryos conceived in glass to her womb should fail. What would be done with the embryos she didn't need, Prof. Silver does not say.

Another emerging technology is embryo biopsy. It is already possible to scrape a few cells off an early embryo, analyze particular genes to see if they are defective (e.g., if they carry an hereditary disease), and then decide whether "to transfer this embryo back into the womb of a gestational mother." Or, if a couple is known to be at risk of passing on an hereditary disease, they could have a pool of embryos conceived *in vitro*. Their physician could then select one of the embryos found to be free of the disease and implant it in the womb; the rest of the embryos presumably would be junked.

A third area in which rapid advance is forseeable is genetic engineering, i.e., injecting a gene from some other source into an embryo. "The most obvious use of this technology in human beings," Prof. Silver remarks, "would be to cure particular diseases through the injection of normal genes into deficient human embryos." But he warns that "genetic engineering is a two-edged sword with a great potential for use and a great potential for abuse," e.g., for producing children with non-human traits.

We must wonder, however, about his norm for deciding what is non-human when we read his speculation on the final technological development, by which human males could become pregnant and carry a child to term. At present, of course, this cannot be done, but there are reasons for thinking it could some day be done: "First, the endocrinology of reproduction is well understood and could be simulated in men. Second, there is no absolute requirement for a uterus to carry out gestation."

But why would a man want to undergo "the drastic physiological changes" necessary to bear a child? Well, he might be a partner in a homosexual union. Or he might be the husband of a woman who is physically unable to sustain a pregnancy, and a surrogate mother might not be available. In that case, the husband might be willing to take his wife's place. "One should be cautious," says Prof. Silver, "not to underestimate the lengths to which infertile couples will go to have a baby."

Which is to say that, if people want something badly enough, we should not deny them the means of getting it. Despite his warnings that some of the things that may be technologically possible would nonetheless be "abuses," or even "outlandish," Prof. Silver offers only a crude utilitarianism as the norm for deciding what would be an abuse. He has destroyed the notion of human nature as the norm, because for him nature is only a manipulable collection of cells.

As C.S. Lewis explained more than forty years ago in *The Abolition of Man*, man's conquest of nature turns out to be the conquest of some men (particularly of those not yet conceived or born) by other men who have lost any idea of a human nature of their own. They have only one word to say to us: plastics.

Dying for Mama

A lady with whom I have long been acquainted told me that at a recent dinner party, an old family friend came up to her and announced: "I think every woman has a right to an abortion if she wants one." She replied, "I think abortion is murder," and walked away. Just as well, too, for he was only looking for an argument and, since he is not one of the brighter lights that gleams amid the encircling gloom, it was not going to be a good one.

But, I thought to myself afterwards, the conversation might have gone like this:

He: I think every woman has a right to an abortion if she wants one.

She: How fortunate for you that your mother didn't exercise that right and abort you.

He: But I was not unwanted. She *wanted* me.

She: Suppose you had been unwanted and she had aborted you at, say, three months, or three weeks, or three days after conception, who would be dead today?

He: I don't get you.

She: Wouldn't the life she ended by abortion have been your life, and wouldn't it be you who were dead today?

He: I suppose so.

She: Have you ever thanked your mother for not aborting you?

He: That would have been indecent. Besides, I can't thank her now; she died some years ago.

She: But you would agree with her having aborted you, if that is what she had decided to do, because you believe she had the right to do it?

He: Absolutely. Every woman has that right.

She: You must have loved your mother very much.

He: How so?

She: Greater love than this no man hath, that he lay down his life for a friend. But it seems to me an even greater love if a son is willing to have laid down his life for his mother's right to abort him.

He: What does love have to do with it? We're talking about rights.

That conversation never took place, of course, and I doubt if it ever would take place in real life. As Plato knew, the advantage of composing a Platonic dialogue is that Plato writes all the lines and can make them come out as he wants them to. Real dialogues seldom come out as either participant planned. Nonetheless, the above dialogue, contrived though it is, does make a valid point.

If you insist on a universal right to abortion, the life that was aborted could have been your own, and the mother who bore you could have been the mother who killed you. Granted, she would have had her reasons (for she was not a capriciously evil woman), but would you have been willing to die for them?

Abortion, after all, involves killing and dying. Technically, it is true, every premature expulsion of a child from the womb is an abortion, and would be an abortion even if removing the child from the womb managed to save its life as well as the mother's. But such an abortion is rare, if it happens at all. It is not the reality we are talking about when we discuss abortion in the contemporary United States.

According to the figure that is now routinely reported in the secular press, there are about one and a half million abortions performed every year in this country, and they terminate from a quarter to a third of all pregnancies. The point of virtually all of them is to kill the baby or, if you insist, to kill the living being in the womb before it becomes a baby. Either way, a human life is deliberately and intentionally ended; if your mother had aborted you before you became a baby, you'd be just as dead. The right to abort is the right to kill, and in abortion as it is actually practiced, a living human being always dies.

The ultimate pro-abortion answer to that proposition is, So what? Take Katha Pollitt, who is identified as "a poet and writer who lives in New York." In a column in *The New York Times Magazine* for November 20, 1988, she argues the pro-abortion case in terms that make it clear that she does not care who or what dies in an abortion.

Let us stop talking, she suggests, only about the hard cases of "pregnant schoolgirls, rape and incest victims," etc., and meet the real issue head-on: "All over the industrialized West, women want education and jobs, couples want small, planned families, and people—men and women, married and unmarried—want sexual intimacy." These "imperatives" are the premises from which all moral reasoning in this area of life must begin, the absolutes to which all other considerations must yield.

We need not pretend that "abortion isn't or shouldn't be a method of birth control." Let us face it, "that's just what abortion is—a bloody, clumsy method of birth control." It is fully justified because the women who resort to it are confronted with "disaster," not "inconvenience": "Women do what they need to do to lead reasonable lives, and they always have. Nowadays, a reasonable life does not include shotgun weddings, or dropping out of school, or embracing the minimum wage for life. Still less does it include bearing a baby for strangers to adopt, as George Bush blithely suggests." In the face of such disasters, "when your back is against the wall of unwanted pregnancy, it doesn't matter whether or not you think the fetus is a person."

That seems clear enough, does it not? Person or not, you kill it when it gets in the way of a reasonable life. But would you still agree with that if the reasonable life were your mother's, and the life she ended were your own?

The Rot in Liberal Politics

Even liberals are beginning to notice what is wrong with liberalism. In a perceptive article which appeared in, of all places, the liberal Catholic journal *Commonweal* (Jan. 13, 1989), Fred Siegel put his finger on contemporary liberalism's Achilles heel. "Liberalism," he says, "has a proud history of defending individual rights. . . . But liberalism, wrapped as it is in the defense of personal autonomy, is unable to speak to the social breakdown which increasingly plagues us. It is mute before abuses of liberty."

"The law," he explains, "once the cornerstone of ordered liberty, has been trivialized, turned into a game for lawyers." There has been "a decisive break between New Deal liberalism, whose mild economic egalitarianism was based on a sense of shared values, and the moral relativism of post-New Deal liberalism which is grounded in individually held rights. Those assertions of rights which serve to trump the claims of a common morality make it difficult and often impossible for cultural liberals to pass judgment on even the most obviously destructive behavior."

There, he says, we may find a major reason for the Democratic Party's defeat in the last presidential election. Since 1968 the party has been preoccupied with procedural rules designed to guarantee proportional representation to all of its constituent groups, however out of harmony with the general electorate they may be. But this preoccupation with procedures is "a means of avoiding a consensus on at least a core of substantive issues. In that sense the Democratic Party's proceduralism is a faithful reflection of contemporary liberalism's unwillingness to pass judgment on what is or isn't good."

Mr. Siegel's purpose in that article was to warn liberals that they are killing the Democratic Party's chances in national elections. But the rot now so apparent in liberal politics was planted in liberal social and political theory at its beginning, more than three centuries ago. Liberalism in its classical form was, and remains today, a radically individualistic philosophy. Even when it veers toward the welfare state or democratic socialism, it does so in order to equalize everyone's chance to live the lifestyle of his choice. It has no theory of what is a good life for human beings as such.

Liberal thought takes as its starting point the discrete individual who is sovereign over himself and a subject of rights prior to all obligations. The problem which liberal political theory thus sets for itself is to explain how and why such an individual entered an organized civil society and subjected himself to government.

He must have acted on motives of self-interest because, as an absolute individual, he had no other motives to act on. His relationships to other individuals and to society must therefore be contractual: his only obligations to them are those to which he has consented, and his motive for consenting must be his belief that he will thereby further his own interests. On these premises, freedom is the right to do one's own will, limited only by the equal right of other individuals to do their will, and the purpose of government is nothing more than to protect these rights.

I read somewhere, not long ago, that liberalism's great accomplishments were to break the power of absolute monarchs, thus bringing governments under law, and to establish religious freedom. One could point out that constitutionalism, the doctrine that government is limited by law, is far older than the rise of liberalism in the seventeenth century. It was in the thirteenth century that Bracton wrote, "The king is under no man, but under God and the law," and that idea was already old when he wrote. But it is true historically that modern conceptions of limited, constitutional government and of religious liberty triumphed in the modern world under the aegis of liberalism.

But much as we may applaud the historical achievements of liberalism, we must also recognize that one of its consequences has been the steady relativization of the ideas of truth and moral good, and that this was a consequence implicit in liberal individualism from the beginning. For multitudes today, truth is only what the individual thinks is true, good is only what the individual personally prefers, and justice is his right to act on his preferences, so long as they are compatible with the equal right of others to do the same.

PINS IN THE LIBERAL BALLOON

That is currently the liberal model of society, and it is falling apart. Constitutional democracy clearly needs a better theoretical foundation than liberal individualism.

It is not that a sounder theory of democracy has yet to be written. We may find powerful essays towards it in John Hallowell's *Moral Foundation of Democracy*, Yves Simon's *Philosophy of Democratic Government*, Jacques Maritain's *Man and the State*, and a host of other books. The major task remaining to us is to persuade the rest of the population—particularly academics, journalists, and lawyers—to stop taking liberalism with its individualism, its relativism, and its assertion of rights that trump the claims of a common morality, as the necessary foundation of democracy. Liberalism, which we may credit with beginning its career as the political philosophy of freedom, has blossomed into mere permissiveness, and is now a menace rather than a support of constitutional democracy.

'And you're sure that you can build all this in one day?'

How to Read a Newspaper

When reading the New York *Times*, one must ask oneself certain questions: Why is the *Times* telling me this? Why does it tell it to me upfront instead of back on page 30? What does the *Times* want me to believe today?

These questions spring to one's mind when reading a news story like the following, which appeared some time ago but is typical of many another. On Sunday, February 5, 1989, on page three of its National Edition, the *Times* carried a report written by one Seth Mydans about Pagsanjan, a town 40 miles southeast of Manila in the Philippines. According to Mr. Mydans, the town flourishes on prostituting boys to homosexuals, many of them visiting or resident foreigners. This trade in young male flesh, he says, is staunchly defended by the town government and the parents of the boys. As a resident who requested anonymity put it, "The moral attitude of the town is pro-prostitution. The attitude is, everyone's doing it, you're not going to get pregnant, and you get the money."

What is going on in Pagsanjan, Mydans reports, can be thoroughly documented by a woman who lives in the town and "will spread on her table hundreds of pictures of local boys performing sexual acts with foreign men, as well as neatly typed index cards with the names of the boys and their customers."

This is interesting and, if true (which I do not question), it is shocking, but is it simply a report on something taking place in an obscure town in a country halfway around the globe, or is something more being conveyed to us? One begins to suspect the latter when one reads the following sentences in the report: "The powerful Roman Catholic Church has had little to say on the subject of prostitution or the exploitation of women and children, in marked contrast to its aggressive stand against artificial birth control. President Corazon C. Aquino, a devout Catholic, also has not made an issue of prostitution, while at the same time avoiding the urgent but controversial problem of population control."

Ah yes, population control through artificial birth control.

It would cure the poverty of the Philippines (and of any other Third World country) and no doubt raise the level of its sexual morals to that of the United States. But it is blocked by a Church that is callously indifferent to the plight of the poor, and by a devout but misguided woman who believes what the Church tells her. Members of the U.S. Congress will please note and remember when voting on foreign aid programs.

So will members of State legislatures, city and county councils, and local school boards. Foreign aid does not fall within their jurisdiction, but public health and sex education programs do, and Planned Parenthood stands ready to help them, if not checked by a certain sinister institution. The scandalous behavior in Pagsanjan, the Philippines, you see, is relevant after all to our American concerns. The sophisticated reader of the *Times* will recognize the message, and the unsophisticated one will get it without realizing that it is a message.

Lest it be thought, however, that editorializing in the news columns is confined to the East Coast, let us mention a story which appeared in California, on page two of the San Jose *Mercury News*. It was hardly a hot-off-the-press story; it began by reporting police raids on an abortion clinic and some doctors' offices in Mexico City on March 16, 1989, but the *Mercury News* did not print it until Tuesday, April 11.

But no matter. The real point of the story, written from Mexico City by Katherine Ellison, was this: "Mexico's abortion law broadly resembles limits advocated in the United States by President George Bush. Under the law, abortions are allowed if the pregnancy could kill the mother or if it has resulted from rape." But Mexican experience shows that George Bush is wrong.

In a section of her story, subheadlined "Illegal abortion horror tales," Ms. Ellison recounts the same sort of statistics and anecdotes about Mexico with which we were deluged about our own country in the years before *Roe v. Wade*. If you were of adult age in the 1960's, you remember them well, and I need not detail them here.

The most important statistic that she alleges is that "every year at least half a million Mexican women deliberately abort their pregnancies. Every year, also, at least 100 of these woman die. . . . The actual toll is much higher, perhaps in the thousands, insist doctors and others who have fought since the 1970's for legal abortions." Near the end of the article we learn that "reports in Mexico continue to state that up to 200,000 women each year die from complications, a number foreign experts call improbable." But, if the number is improbable, why report it? Perhaps in the hope that the inflated figure will be the one that sticks in your mind. You must be made to understand that Mexico is faced with a Holocaust, not of babies like the more than 20 million we have aborted in the United States since *Roe v. Wade*, but of women who have died from illegal abortions.

And who is to blame for this? Ms. Ellison lays it on the line: "The search for a secret abortion, and the costs and risks of getting one are common trials for women of all economic classes in this Catholic nation." Mexico has an anti-clerical constitution and a record of persecuting the Church. "Yet Mexico is overwhelmingly a Catholic country. Top leaders go faithfully to Mass, priests have a strong, if subtle, influence, and laws reflect conservative morality."

The experienced reader asks himself why the *Mercury News* chose this moment to publish this report. He recalls that it appeared on April 11, two days after the Great Big Pro-Abortion Rally in Washington, D.C., which was meant to warn the U.S. Supreme Court that it had better not tamper with *Roe v. Wade*. Then it occurs to him that, just possibly, the *Mercury News* was helping the cause along with anti-Catholic horror stories from Mexico.

An Uncertain Trumpet

There has been a sharp drop in vocations to the Catholic priesthood since Vatican II. One of the reasons for it may be confusion among priests themselves about what the priestly vocation is.

We have long had clerics who do not think that gaiety should be confined to the laity, and who therefore have dedicated their lives to fighting Jansenism by both word and example. Now we have priests who take it as their mission to relieve Catholics of their hangups on faith and morals by telling them how much of what the Church teaches they need not believe or do. Still others devote themselves to solving people's problems by, for example, finding ways for them to remarry after divorce. Yet others again concentrate on society's larger problems, and try to solve them through political action.

Some priests, particularly young ones, seem to be dubious about the significance of their own priesthood. I recall a concelebration of the Mass in which I once took part. The principal celebrant delivered a homily on the eucharist in which there was much talk of bread and wine, but little, if any, of the Body and Blood of Christ. He referred to himself, along with the rest of us on the altar, as "presiding at the eucharistic liturgy." What that meant was not clear, since "eucharist" seemed to be a warm and fuzzy feeling that embraced everyone and everything. But whatever it was, we were presiding at it.

Although there were at least fifteen priests on the altar, when it came time to distribute communion, that task was performed by a team of lay ministers, most of them women. It occurred to me, as I watched this, that if I were trying to attract young men to the priesthood, I would not go about it in this way.

But, of course, trying to attract young men to the priesthood is a sexist, pre-Vatican II idea rooted in an outdated ecclesiology. Since, as we now see, our real religion is democracy, and democracy means equality, recruitment to the priesthood must aim at women as well as men.

The priesthood to which we are to admit women, however, may not be what Catholics have previously understood the priesthood to be. Some years ago, for instance, I attended a symposium—more like a pep rally, as it turned out—on the ordination of women. The last speaker of the evening was a lady who since then has achieved a certain prominence as a newspaper reporter. But that evening she was a theologian, and offered a theological argument which in effect abolished the priesthood.

The conclusion toward which her argument steadily moved was that no one should be ordained, because the congregation does everything that is done in the liturgy. At the last minute, however, she remembered that she was there to argue for the ordination of women, so she concluded that women should be ordained. When she finished, I turned to an Episcopalian friend who was sitting next to me and said, "That lady may not know it, but she is not a Catholic." "Of course," he agreed, "that was straight Congregationalist theology."

I don't doubt but that some of those who advocate the ordination of women want them to be ordained to the traditional, sacramental Catholic priesthood. Others, however, seem to want to do away with that "magical" and "hocus-pocus" conception of the role of the priest. Not only does it elevate men above women, it confers on the clergy the privilege of exercising a divine power which is denied to lay people. But to give to some what others cannot have is to exclude the latter, and the idea of exclusion is offensive to pious democratic ears.

When someone brings up the subject of the priesthood, therefore, it is advisable to ask, What priesthood do you have in mind? It may be only a priesthood in which all can share because it can do nothing that any Christian cannot do. But then, is there anything Christians can do that non-Christians cannot also do? Must we not rather say that all of us, whether we know it or not—indeed, whether we want it or not—are children of the One God and can serve equally as instruments in His or Her hands, without distinction of race, sex, or creed?

I know it sounds strange, but it is a fact, easily documented, that there is a certain amount of speculation in Catholic theological circles which questions not only the exclusive functions of the priesthood, but the exclusive claims of Christianity itself. We may no longer hold, these writers tell us, that Christ is uniquely the way, the truth, and the life; that no one comes to the Father but through Him; and that there is no other name than His under heaven given unto men by which we must be saved. God wants all men to be saved, and all sincere ways of seeking Him will lead us to salvation.

There is enough truth in that to make it an effective piece of sophistry. It is true that God gives every human being sufficient grace to be saved, and condemns no one for inculpable ignorance. But to draw the conclusion that therefore there is no one true religion is to reject Christianity with its undeniable exclusivist claim to be the saving truth revealed by God.

The number of priests who go that far is very small, but a larger number are manifestly uneasy about "triumphalist" claims to possession of the truth. The more widespread that attitude becomes among the clergy, however, the more difficult it will be to attract recruits to the Catholic priesthood. For if the trumpet gives forth an uncertain sound, who will gird himself for battle?

The Truth about Christmas

Christmas is a scandal to the modern mind. It is not only that it has a child being born to a virgin; the greater scandal is that it has him born at all, as God entering the human race through a woman's womb. Christmas celebrates the birth of the incarnate God to a human mother whose name we know (Mary) in a place that is still there (Bethlehem), at an identifiable time in human history (when Caesar Augustus ruled the Roman Empire and Quirinius was governor of Syria). This immersion of God in historical particularity offends a mind for which, if there is a God, He should be above all that.

The Christ whose birth Christmas commemorates is presented to us as an historical figure who lived a real life in the real world, and at the end of that life was crucified, died, and rose again from the dead. The Resurrection too, however, along with all the miracles in between, is intolerable to a certain type of intellectual who wants his religion reduced to a set of "meanings" unencumbered by embarrassing assertions of fact that cannot be true and must be taken as mythological.

That Jesus was born of a virgin mother is therefore translated into a symbolic way of saying that he was an important person. That he rose again from the dead is not denied—at least, not by theologians who want to go on teaching in Catholic faculties of theology—but it is "reinterpreted" in such a way as to take it out of history. To give but one recent example, the magazine *30 Days* for September 1989, quotes the Rev. David Coffey, president of the Australian Catholic Theological Association, as saying that "the resurrection is an event of grace not involving in any way the corpse of Jesus."

We must hold, that is to say, that Jesus in some sense rose from the dead (the Creeds force us to admit that much), but his dead body did not come back to life. The historical event of his death was not followed by the equally historical event of his returning to life in the body that died on the cross. Science tells us that a corpse cannot live again, and Fr. Coffey assures us that only "in a pre-scientific age" could one believe that a corpse did that. While we must believe in the resurrection, therefore, we must also believe that it means something other than that the dead body of Jesus rose again to physical life in this world.

If this kind of theological thinking is carried all the way through, it ultimately calls into question the Incarnation itself, for it must seem strange that we can believe that God became man, but not that He was born of a virgin or that He rose from the dead. Liberal Christianity tends inexorably, as its history shows, toward Unitarianism, for which, as the quip has it, there is but one God at most. It not only takes Christ out of Christmas, it takes Him out of history altogether. All that is left in the real world in which history actually took place is the man called Jesus who lived, taught, and was executed in Palestine two thousand years ago. The rest of the Christian faith is imaginative symbolism designed to convey insights into the human condition to a myth-making age. But in our age, whose only mythology is Science, the historical Christian faith just won't do.

The outburst of art, music, and liturgy that Christmas has produced during the Christian centuries was hardly inspired by this anemic and insubstantial liberal Christianity. People do not go to midnight Mass to celebrate a birth that is merely symbolic of whatever philosophical beliefs happen to be fashionable in theological faculties. Nor do men and women become Christians if that is all that Christianity has to offer. As C. S. Lewis wrote to his friend, Malcolm, "did you ever meet, or hear of, anyone who was converted from scepticism to a 'liberal' or 'de-mythologized' Christianity? I think when unbelievers come in at all, they come in a good deal further."

Christmas is a season of joy because the Feast of the Nativity gives us something of supreme importance to rejoice about. It presupposes that we are a fallen race because of a real original sin, from the consequences of which we all need to be saved. Sin is not a popular subject, even in sermons, in an age in which religion is more and more a psychotherapy aimed at making people feel good about themselves. Yet we cannot fail to notice that the greatest horrors of our time are not the San Francisco earthquake, or Hurricane Hugo, or the tornado that ravaged Huntsville, Alabama. The worst evils we suffer are the ones we inflict on one another, on a scale we would consider massive if we had not become inured to it by seeing it every evening on the TV news.

We—all of us, and not only the obvious and flagrant bad guys—are weak, prone to sin, and in need of salvation. Without that conviction, Christmas makes no sense and gives us little joy. We rejoice because the real God became a real man and offered His life in expiation for our real sins, thereby giving us the chance to escape a real damnation and to win eternal life in a real heaven.

The tidings of great joy at Christmas are that "this day is born unto you in the city of David a Savior, who is Christ the Lord." With that announcement, Christ was born into this world. His last words to His apostles on leaving it were: "Go, therefore, and teach all nations, baptizing them in the name of the Father, and of the Son and of the Holy Spirit, . . . and lo, I am with you always even to the end of the world." Christ carries on His saving mission in historical time through His Church, and will carry it on until history comes to its appointed close.

All of these beliefs are implied in Christmas. If they are not true, the birth of Jesus from Mary in Bethlehem is insignificant. But if they are true, it is the most blessed event in history, on which the whole meaning of history turns. We have to take our Christianity straight, or it is not worth taking at all.

The Devil We Know

John Cardinal O'Connor, the Archbishop of New York, created something of a sensation earlier this year with a Sunday sermon in his cathedral on the subject of Satanism. He got headlines for denouncing an increase in Satanic practices which he said were encouraged, particularly among teenagers, by heavy-metal rock music. What most grabbed attention, however, was his evident belief that Satan truly existed and that there are real, though rare, instances of demonic possession that require exorcism.

The press at once telephoned a number of experts for opinions on the Cardinal's sermon, including those theologians who can be counted on to give a modernist answer to any question. Thus *Time* reported on March 19, 1990:

> Father Richard McBrien, chairman of the theology department at the University of Notre Dame, dismisses the idea of a personal archdemon as "premodern and precritical." Individuals tend to personify evil, he explains, "because we see it in people." But for sophisticates acquainted with sociology and other disciplines, says McBrien, "sin is now seen as something systemic, institutional and structural, as well as personal."

When I myself am asked if I believe in a personal devil, I always reply: "Of course. How else could one account for the liberal mind?" As you may imagine, this answer is not well received by sophisticates acquainted with sociology and other disciplines, and I must admit that it is a bit flippant. I am not concerned here, however, to defend my belief, but to ask another and more important question: Why is it taken for granted that, in the modern world, no intelligent person can believe in a personal spirit of evil or in non-human spirits of any kind?

For example, on the TV program *The McLaughlin Group*, moderator John McLaughlin asked a panel of four men what they thought of Cardinal O'Connor's sermon. Two of them dismissed it out of hand, but the other two were unwilling to do that. There is a spirit of evil in the world, they said, some rock music panders to it, and we should recognize Satanism as capable of doing genuine harm to young people—but they did not regard this spirit of evil as a person.

But how do we know that unseen personal agents do not act on human beings to tempt them to evil? To reject that possibility seems strange in Christians who profess to believe that the unseen grace of God is indispensable for good deeds and the avoidance of sin, and that unless God acts within us to enlighten our minds and move our wills, we cannot faithfully serve Him. What, then, makes them so sure that all impulses to evil arise solely from ourselves? Is it really obvious to any thinking man that the horrors of the twentieth century are attributed exclusively to the base inclinations of the human heart?

To push the question further, is our understanding of the human psyche so exhaustive that we can fully explain all the motives that actuate human beings? Well, no, we have to admit that much work remains to be done in the science of psychology. But we must also insist that it is a science and that, in principle, it can explain the whole of human motivation. We may therefore be confident that some day it will do so, because what science cannot, even in principle, explain is not real.

This attitude reflects a certain view of the world that is derived from the spectacular triumphs of science in early modern times, which have continued to the present day. Science not only explains the world, it will eventually explain it entirely. Seen in this perspective, the world is a vast and complicated machine in which everything that happens can be reduced to prior and knowable causes. In such a machine we know that everything has a "natural" explanation, and there is no room for "supernatural," personal, non-mechanical causes.

But, of course, we do not *know* that; we can only believe it. Scientism, that belief that all phenomena, including human actions, can be explained by the method of the natural sciences, is as much a faith as any taught by a church. It is no less a faith because the multitudes who have been raised in it take it as unquestionable scientific truth. They rely, as Thomas Spragens remarks in his *The Irony of Liberal Reason*, "on a credulous interpretation of scientific reason that has become the principal superstition of modernity." Those who are steeped in this superstition reject diabolic possession, not because there is no evidence for it, but because they are convinced that the evidence must have some natural explanation.

Will Rogers used to say, "The trouble with this country is that too many people know too many things that just ain't so." Our problem is not that we do not believe enough, but that we believe far too much, on no better ground than that it is what "everybody knows." A certain skepticism is therefore in order for men and women of Christian faith. Sheldon Vanauken has put it well in his *Under the Mercy*: "There is only one wisdom for Christians: to look with a cool and very skeptical eye at all the things their own age is precisely *most certain* of. Especially is this true of the certainties that contradict what has been believed by wise Christians down the centuries."

Wise Christians have believed down the centuries in fallen angels. We may therefore do so, too, and need not be overly impressed by theological sophisticates. After all, as the Anglican writer, Harry Blamires, has said, "We do not need a horned devil, scattering lies, to lead us astray. A theologian, speaking selected truths, can do it just as easily." Especially if the theologian doesn't believe in the devil.

Doing Better for Lent

In the coming season of Lent, the Church will ask us to reflect upon our sins and to do penance for them. While we are so engaged, we may also spare a thought for the dry rot that afflicts us collectively as the church in this country.

We may notice, for instance, that Lenten exhortations to do penance for our sins are not widely heeded among Catholics, because the sense of sin has faded among us, as it has among so many other people in the modern world. We may even be struck by the absence of Lenten exhortations, since the clergy are reluctant to upset us, or themselves for that matter.

In St. Mark's gospel (2:18-20), people asked Our Lord, "Why do John's disciples and the disciples of the Pharisees fast, but your disciples do not fast?" He replied, "Can the wedding guests fast while the bridegroom is with them? . . . The day will come when the bridegroom will be taken away from them, and then they will fast on that day."

That day has come, and has gone. Fasting in Lent was once a common Catholic practice, but no longer. Why, after all, should those who are not conscious of sin feel the need for penance? Even in some religious houses, no provision is made in the menu for those who might want to keep the Lenten fast. In the clerical circles in which I move, it is customary to joke about the ridiculous preoccupation we used to have with precisely how many ounces of food one could eat in a fast-day meal. We have got rid of that kind of scrupulosity, but we have done it by dropping fasting and the very idea of physical penance.

This shift of consciousness among Catholics helps to explain the phenomenon of whole congregations receiving communion at Mass, even though most of them have not bothered to confess their sins or felt the need to do so. It also explains the demand for general absolution without the bothersome need for individual confession to a priest who might not agree with one's personal moral code. It throws light, too, on the outrage felt by liberal clerics when reactionary pastors announce from the pulpit that only Catholics should come forward for communion. For many Catholics, it is apparent, the eucharist has become a mere ritual, not a sacrament to be taken with utmost reverence.

The fading sense of sin also shows up in the growing Catholic acceptance of contraception, abortion, and divorce, and in our more tolerant attitude toward pornography, pre- and extra-marital sex, and homosexuality as an alternative lifestyle. The Catholic Church has always been keenly aware that ours is a fallen human nature, to the point where it sometimes scandalized pious Protestants by its readiness to forgive sins. The post-Christian world, however, is not only aware of fallen human nature but takes it as normative. Today, doing what comes naturally is not only what people do but what they have a right to do, and it is considered arrogant and unfeeling to ask them to do more than keep their quest for self-gratification within the bounds of moderation. That so many Catholics now take the same view of human nature reveals the dry rot that is eating away at the life of the Church.

For Christianity means nothing if it does not mean salvation from sin and from the disordered passions that lead to it. In the Christian view of man, all is not right with us, our nature is deeply wounded, and we need the constant help of divine grace through the Mass, the sacraments, prayer, and the practice of a Christian spirituality to live in a manner pleasing to God, and so to save our souls.

Catholics by and large once knew all that, even when they did not try to live it. But Christendom, the society in which Christianity could be taken for granted, has ended, has been coming to an end, in fact, for at least 300 years. With its final disappearance, we shall soon also see no more merely nominal or post-Christian Catholics. The gap between Catholicism and the general culture will be so wide and so inescapably visible that we shall all have to take our stand on one or the other side of it.

Critics may say that the only moral decline I can point to (if it is a decline) is in sexual morals, and that today's Catholics are in fact better in other areas of life than earlier generations were—less racist, for example. But the sexually liberated Catholic who is a model of self-sacrificing Christian charity is a pipe dream. Conforming to the sexual mores of the post-Christian culture may make us more easy-going, tolerant liberal democrats, but it won't make us better Christians or even better citizens.

The end of Christendom will also manifest itself, as it is already doing, in the decay from within of Catholic institutions. In the larger Catholic colleges and universities, Catholicism will fade away like the Cheshire cat, leaving behind only a bland, reassuring, administrative smile. A similar process will take place in Catholic hospitals and social-welfare agencies, as both their personnel and the norms by which they are forced to operate become more and more secularized.

A magazine recently asked a number of prominent people, "What's Your Best Hope for the 1990s?" Walker Percy's answer was, "There will occur the spread of democratic societies, but of a certain sort: deeply informed by the values of the visual media, violence, pornography, standard network Brokaw-Rather ideology, Hollywood morality, and 10,000 Japanese car commercials. My hope is that we might do better." This Lent, let us hope the same for the American Catholic Church.

Handling the Easy Cases

What would I do about abortion if I had the power? The first answer to that question is that I don't have that power, I am never going to have it, and I don't want it. In a constitutional democracy, no one, and no single group of persons, has the power to make and enforce laws. Under a constitution and within its bounds, democratic government is government by the consent of the people acting by majority, which is presumed to be the larger and sounder part of the people, at least in the long run.

That consideration should take care of the liberal cant about not imposing our moral beliefs on others. I cannot impose my moral beliefs on anyone, and most certainly not living, as I do, in the City of New York, where no candidate has a chance of election to high public office unless he lays his hand on his heart and vows never to do anything to restrict in any way the sacred right to abortion. Nor could all American Catholics together impose their beliefs on an unwilling people, even if we were a monolithic bloc, as we obviously are not.

Let us rephrase the question, then. What would I do about abortion if I were in high public office as, say, the governor of a state or the mayor of a city, or the majority leader of one of the houses of a state legislature? I would carry the people with me as far as I could persuade them to go in restricting abortion. More than that I could not do, and my task would be one of persuasion, not of imposition.

I don't mean, of course, that I could do nothing until I had persuaded Molly Yard, or the American Civil Liberties Union, or the editorial board of the New York *Times*. They are only part of the American people, and not by definition the larger and sounder part. Like the rest of us, all they can do is to try to persuade their fellow citizens, at least if the U.S. Supreme Court follows through on the indication it gave last summer that it is now willing to let the people have something to say on the legality of abortion.

In my effort to persuade, I would begin at the beginning, not at the end. I would not start, that is, by proposing a constitutional amendment to prohibit or restrict abortion. Such a proposal will be successful, if ever, only at the end of a long process of getting the American people to face and to think seriously about what abortion is and what we have done (or have had done to us) by the present legalization of abortion on demand.

To begin at the beginning is to talk about the existing situation: one and a half million abortions every year, which terminate almost a third of all pregnancies, and have killed more than 20 million babies since *Roe v. Wade*. If I were asked, as I surely would be, what I would do about pregnancies due to rape or incest, I would reply by asking another question: Are you willing to do anything to reduce the 1.5 million abortions performed in this country every year?

If not, why not? Even according to Planned Parenthood's research arm, the Alan Guttmacher Institute, rape and incest account for only about one per cent of all abortions; they are not the major issue in the abortion controversy. If, however, you agree that abortion on demand should be reduced, then work with us to put some effective limits on it. When we get to the end of the line and face the "hard cases," we can disagree—but let's get there first and, in the meantime, stop talking as if rape and incest were the only reasons for abortion.

One advantage of beginning at the beginning is that it breaks the abortion issue down into more specific issues on which it is possible to get the people to suppport legislation. William McGurn has explained in *National Review* (December 22, 1989):

> Most Amercians would be suspicious of a politician who favored allowing their 13-year-old daughters to have abortions without the parents' consent when these same girls can't get their ears pierced without parental permission. Most Americans would look askance at a candidate who opposed giving American women the same extensive information about abortion that they can get on every other operation. Most Americans would be horrified by a candidate who believed it was okay for someone to have an abortion if she was hoping for a boy and proved to be carrying a girl. Most Americans would not give their vote to someone who argued for abortion into the late stages of pregnancy. Above all, most Americans would find something extreme in a party that was shown to oppose all these restrictions on abortion.

The second and more important advantage of taking this

approach is that it keeps the abortion issue alive. Abortion is at bottom not merely a legal, or even a constitutional issue, but a moral one. Richard John Neuhaus has concisely stated it in the new monthly journal, *First Things*: "Who shall live? Who shall die? Who does, and who does not, belong to the community for which we accept common responsibility?" That is an issue of the most profound *public* moral importance.

But it would fade out of the consciousness of many people as an issue of public morality if we passively accepted the present legal situation, in which abortion is a purely private choice. To keep it in the public forum as a moral issue that involves the community as such, it is necessary to make it a legal and therefore a political issue, however much politicians wish it would go away. To make it a political issue, it is further necessary to propose the kind of legislation to which the larger and sounder part of the people are now, at this moment, willing to agree, and with which politicians will find it difficult to disagree. When the leaders of the people won't lead, the people have to get behind and push them.

All of This for Me

I stopped the other day at a traffic light in the Bronx and read the bumper sticker on the car in front of me. "Life is tough," it proclaimed, "then you die."

It was a view of life, I am sure, as fully entitled to expression as any other in this land of liberty. Considering the circumstances in which many people in the Borough of the Bronx live, it was even an understandable one. Yet it is strangely popular among people who are neither poor nor denizens of the Bronx.

Take for example Samuel Beckett's *Waiting for Godot*, the message of which is that, if we wait for God to come to us, we'll wait forever. It was recently revived for a limited run in New York. Liz Smith of the New York *Daily News* commented that years ago, when Bert Lahr starred in the play, "people all went around saying they didn't understand it." But "nowadays Beckett's play doesn't seem a bit strange or difficult. The world has grown into his existentialist, nihilistic viewpoint." Liz Smith is not a trained sociologist, but a gossip columnist. Yet her naively sophisticated remark is probably accurate. The world in which she moves has "grown into" acceptance of Beckett's bleak message.

Or, at least, that part of her world that understands the message accepts it. There are surely those who go to see Beckett's play merely because it is a current sensation. Such questions as whether the universe was created by a loving God, or has existed by and of itself from all eternity seem to them to be irrelevant to the practical concerns of real life. After all, if you are running a business, you don't ask your employees or your customers what they think of the universe.

Yet our view of the universe has a real influence on how we live our lives. If there is no God, or if God is indifferent to us and our fate, then we are alone in the universe, simply and totally on our own.

The desire to be on our own has been one of the great driving forces of modern thought. Millions of our fellow human beings have yielded to it, and more are joining them every year. I read recently that a poll taken in Europe purports to reveal that, while the vast majority of Europeans still profess to believe in God, a diminishing proportion of them see Him as "personal." Life seems to them to be easier and less ridden by anxiety and guilt if they don't have to worry about what God thinks of them, and an impersonal God doesn't think, certainly not about individual human beings and their sins.

We can take life on those terms, I suppose, so long as we are healthy, prosperous, and able to do as we please. That may account for the popularity of Beckett's view of the world among those who can afford to buy theater tickets in New York.

Yet even they may at times be troubled by the thought that life is ultimately meaningless. If one is sufficiently young and not overly bright, of course, one can screen out that thought. But as we come against the disappointments, failures, miseries, and tragedies that are an inescapable fact of life, we are forced to ask ourselves whether we can handle our lives completely on our own, and we may begin to wonder whether a life that is lost in a meaningless cosmos is worth living.

The answer that the Christian faith gives to those questions at Christmas is a startling one. In his *Spiritual Exercises*, St. Ignatius Loyola has a meditation on the birth of Christ in Bethlehem. At the end of the meditation, he asks us to reflect that Jesus was born there "in dire poverty, so that after many labors, hunger and thirst, heat and cold, injuries and insults, he might die on the cross, and all of this for me."

And all of this for me. Now, there is a radically different view of life: God loves me, individually and personally, and was even willing to become man and die for me. He not only loves all of us collectively, as the Creator of the human race, He loves each one of us individually. Most strange of all, He loves *me*. That is hard to believe, but it is precisely that which the feast of Christmas asks us to believe.

This belief, in one respect, does not change the world at all. Life is still tough, or at least it can and will be tough in one way or another, and we all sooner or later die. But the belief that God loves us makes an enormous difference in how we take life. For what we believe changes the world as we see and understand it.

What some see only as the inexorable grinding on of an indifferent universe, we see as the mysterious providence of God guiding us onward to Himself. A created world is a vastly different place from an uncreated one, and a redeemed world is more different still. A personal God who knows, loves, and cares for us is a different God from an impersonal force in the universe. Life in the created and redeemed world may be hard, and often is, but it is not meaningless and hopeless, we are not alone and helpless, and death is not simply the end.

Those are the tidings of comfort and joy that the Christmas carols celebrate, the reason why they greet us with "God rest you merry, gentlemen, let nothing you dismay." If we can find nothing in the carols but beautiful traditional music, we may send Season's Greetings cards to our friends and present them as gifts with the collected works of Friedrich Nietzsche or, if we can get them, tickets to *Waiting for Godot*. But if we accept, and understand, and feel within ourselves the reality of Christ's birth as God's entrance into our human world, we can truly rejoice. For that birth means, to each one of us, that God loves me.